# DISGUISED

Pat Moore as a "middle income lady" with physical constraints.
(Photo by Bruce Byers.)

# DISGUISED

# PAT MOORE

WITH

# CHARLES PAUL CONN

**WORD BOOKS**
PUBLISHER
WACO, TEXAS

A DIVISION OF
WORD, INCORPORATED

DISGUISED!

**Library of Congress Cataloging in Publication Data**

Moore, Pat.
　Disguised!

　1. Moore, Pat.　2. Gerontologists—United States—
Biography.　3. Old age—Social aspects.　4. Aged—
United States—Psychology.　I. Conn, Charles Paul.
II. Title.
HQ1064.U5M674　1985　　　305.2′6′0924　　85–22782
ISBN 0–8499–0516–8

Printed in the United States of America
567898　FG　987654321

To
My Grandfather Dutch,
with my love

# PROLOGUE

It is an early autumn afternoon, 1980, in New York City. The sun shines warmly over Gramercy Park, but a hint of chill in the air signals that the long, muggy days of summer are gone for another year. The sun feels good to the children who play in the park; they run and shout and shed their sweaters onto the shrubbery or the laps of their mothers.

Three *old* women sit quietly on a bench, watching the children play. They sit side by side, and it is apparent they are comfortable together. Unlike the younger women in the park, there seems no need to fill the spaces between them with words. They watch the children playing and the businessmen walking briskly past with brief cases and rolled-up newspapers, and occasionally they talk. For the most part, however, they simply sit and enjoy the late-season sun and the presence of each other. They are friends and it is enough.

The sun loses its grip on the sky and begins a steady slide behind the Manhattan buildings that border Gramercy Park to the west. It is only 4:15 in the afternoon; there is no change in the light, but the loss of the sun brings immediate, if subtle, change in the air as the October chill asserts itself. The children do not notice it, nor do their mothers or the passersby, but the three *old* women on the green bench pull sweaters more tightly around them and rise, as if a bell has rung, somewhere, for all of them. They stand and smooth their dresses and, with no visible farewells, walk slowly away, two of them heading across the park toward Second Avenue, and the third taking a path in the opposite direction.

The woman who walks alone is short and bent. Her pace is agonizingly slow as she uses a cane to negotiate the rutted sidewalk along Eighteenth Street. Judging by her wrinkled face and gray-white hair, her arthritic posture and movement, and her general appearance, she seems well past the age of seventy—more like eighty, maybe even eighty-five. She wears a plain cotton dress and a thin sweater, with a shawl pulled over her shoulders. Her legs are a bit swollen; the shoes are typical orthopedic black. The overall effect is one of well-groomed, though somewhat faded, gentility.

The woman comes to the intersection of Eighteenth Street and First Avenue. Using her cane for support, she steps carefully from the curb to the pavement as the light blinks green. The noise of the traffic is loud, and she seems small and slow against a background of clamor and movement. Younger, taller, busier people brush past her to hurry through the intersection.

She does not hurry. She is the last pedestrian to cross and does not quite reach the other side before the light changes again, causing a yellow taxi, edging impatiently into a left-hand turn, to wait momentarily as she mounts the curb. Safely on the sidewalk, she turns back toward the traffic and smiles at the cabbie, as if to thank him for not honking. It is a fleeting exchange of kindness; it is over in a millisecond, and the woman turns and shuffles on her way.

Any person on Eighteenth Street that day paying any attention at all to the white-haired lady with cane and shawl would assume her to be a typical senior citizen of eighty years, someone's grandmother or great-grandmother.

It would be a reasonable assumption, but it would be completely wrong.

The woman's name is Patricia Moore. Her friends call her Pattie. She is bright and healthy and very attractive. And her age? Barely twenty-six.

If that is true, one might ask, what is this Patricia Moore doing hobbling along a Manhattan sidewalk, stooped and wrinkled, appearing for all the world to be three times her actual age? Why does she not stride vigorously down the street, making trendy small talk with people her own age? Why not a Gucci handbag rather than that cane? Can't she find Ferragamo loafers to replace those scuffed orthopedic lace-ups? And contact lenses instead of those awful glasses?

Why is Pat Moore, age twenty-six, doing this?

The answer to that question is what this book is about. It is the story of a talented young industrial designer who was so intrigued by the lifestyle of older Americans that for a three-year period she virtually became one. It is a story of one woman's journey into her future.

\*   \*   \*   \*

Meeting Pat Moore today, one has difficulty imagining that she ever engaged in such an audacious change of roles. She is the model of a successful young professional woman; she radiates vitality and energy. There is nothing *"old"* about Pat Moore.

Nor is she an actress, or a social worker. Her decision to assume the persona of a woman three times her age emerged from a less likely background—that of industrial design. Pat is an industrial designer, one of few women to find success in this highly competitive and traditionally male-dominated career. She is president of her own design firm, Moore and Associates, which serves major corporate clients all around the country from its offices in downtown New York.

Industrial design is a specialty area which, to the layman, seems to fall somewhere between art and engineering. Industrial designers develop the concepts and products by which we live our everyday lives. Virtually every package we open, every tool we use, every piece of equipment or furniture we own, reaches us by way of some industrial designer's drawing board.

Pat Moore grew up in a working-class home in Buffalo, New York. From the time anyone can remember, she was an exceptional artist. Even as a preschooler, she gravitated toward drawing and painting. Her father gave her a drawing board with paper and a tin can full of crayons, and the family soon came to regard art as "Pattie Anne's special gift."

The Albright Art Museum in Buffalo had a special tutorial art program for elementary school children in those days, and Pat's mother, who was a school-teacher, seized the opportunity for her precocious child. Together, they went by bus to the museum, changing buses three times on the way and again three times on the way back. There, art majors from the University of Buffalo and State Teachers College conducted three-hour classes for Pat and the other children. Mrs. Moore would spend the time shopping, or reading, or just waiting, then take Pat home again on those three buses.

It was during that time that Pat decided she wanted to be an artist; going to New York City and making it as an artist became her single, shining ambition.

Her ability to draw guaranteed Pat the favor of teachers and fellow students throughout high school. At prom time, she was the one who designed and decorated the gym for the big dance. And she was the one in charge of getting the school's float ready for the St. Patrick's Day Parade. She also entered many art contests and won several awards for her work. Then with high school behind her, Pat was college-bound to prepare for a career in art.

Rochester Institute of Technology (RIT) was only an hour's drive from Buffalo and had an art school with a nationwide reputation. It was an obvious choice for Pat and the only college to which she applied. She drove to Rochester with her father for a personal interview, a bulging portfolio of high school art under her arm, and was accepted on the spot.

Like most young artists, Pat originally envisioned a career as a painter. "As a teenager," she recalls, "I would sit in the museum and look at Gauguin's *The Yellow Christ*, and I knew I wanted to leave something behind that would mean as much to people as that painting did to me." But Pat Moore is nothing if not pragmatic, and she soon realized there were few career opportunities in painting and illustration.

During her freshman year, she found her niche in industrial design. A professor told her she would be good at it, and challenged her to try. There were very few women in the field, he cautioned, but if she were good enough to compete, it was the fastest track to travel in the world of art. With that nudge, Pat plunged into a major in industrial design and found it almost perfectly matched to her abilities and temperament.

In 1974 she graduated with a B.F.A. (Bachelor of Fine Arts) degree and entered the job market with a basketful of glowing recommendations from her professors. Immediately she landed one of the top prizes available to a young designer: a job with the prestigious firm of Raymond Loewy.

The Loewy firm was, in the mid–1970s, one of the largest in New York City. With offices at Park Avenue and Fifty-ninth Street, a renowned staff of over one hundred designers, and the near-legendary figure of Raymond Loewy as its founder, the firm represented the top of the heap in New York design circles. For Pat a job at Loewy seemed like a ticket to heaven.

Her first assignment was a project to design the interior of a new automobile for the Soviet Union. As the most junior member of the firm, and one of only three women designers, Pat arrived at Loewy with the aggressiveness of someone who felt the need to prove herself, and soon attracted the attention of top management with her creative ideas. Her next project was a 116–passenger hydrofoil, also for the Soviets, and as she worked on it, she became increasingly concerned about the emphasis being placed on the hydrofoil's style, rather than on the comfort and convenience of the passengers. She realized they were designing a vehicle that worked well for the young, fully functioning adult, but that various areas of the hydrofoil, as in the automobile she had developed, were totally unsuited for older, less dexterous passengers.

The bathrooms, for example, were not easily manageable for older people. She thought of her own favorite grandfather back home in Buffalo—"Dutch," the grandkids called him—and realized that he simply could not function in that hydrofoil.

Thinking of Dutch as the person who would ultimately use the products she designed was a turning point in Pat's career. It was a mental catalyst which triggered an entirely different way of looking at her work. "How would this work for Dutch?" became the question which framed every design decision she made.

Pat Moore wrote a memo. It eventually reached the office of Raymond Loewy himself. "Give me time off from the job to think, to study, to learn more about individualizing the environment for people," the memo requested. "Let me find out more about the older consumer, about the aging process and how it relates to the products we are developing here at Loewy." She was savvy enough to know that she had to develop a market-sensitive rationale for pursuing the needs of the older citizen, that no company would do it from sheer altruism.

So that was the basis of her appeal: learning about and designing for the millions of people out there like Dutch is good business; it makes sense on the bottom line. Pat apparently made a good case because Loewy management opened the door for her to return to school to study biomechanics (the discipline that combines the needs of consumers with the design and ingenuity of products and the environment) and gerontology (the discipline that examines the social, mental, and physical aspects of people throughout their lifespan). Not only did Loewy give her the opportunity to continue her education, but they encouraged her to apply what she learned to the design projects in progress at the firm.

Without having intended to do so, and almost without realizing it was happening, Patricia Moore had begun a trip that, before it was over, would find her lying on a sidewalk in Harlem, beaten and bleeding, wearing the face and the clothes of a very *old* woman.

\*    \*    \*    \*

Two other factors unrelated to her career as an industrial designer influenced Pat's decision to become personally involved in the concerns of older Americans.

One of these is a strong, intensely personal brand of what some would regard as old-fashioned religious faith. Reared in a devout Christian home, she has seen the faith she was taught as a child tested and strained

# CHAPTER

—— **1** ——

MY FRIENDS ASK ME, "WHERE DID YOU GET this crazy idea, Pattie?" I'm still amazed at how quickly and naturally the idea came together, once it began to germinate. It was one of those things that seemed so obvious, once it occurred to me, that I wondered why I had not thought of it long before.

I was walking along the sidewalk, uptown near the Columbia University campus. I had just come from a lecture and was heading down Broadway toward the subway station on 116th Street. My mind was still on the class, on the living conditions of those 25 million Americans that the rest of society calls "elderly."

I remember looking down at my feet as I walked and thinking how much different the simple act of walking along the street must be for me at age twenty-six than if I were age eighty. The shoes would be different, the length of my stride, the way people greeted me as I passed. I remember feeling the futility of reading and talking about what it was like to be *old*, but not being able really to know.

How would it feel to be eighty or eighty-five, I wondered? And how can I ever know, since part of being *old* is the way other people respond to you, and I would have to wait many years to experience that. The idea at first was little more than an intellectual frustration; it was a kind of Catch-22: to understand aging, I must grow older and experience it, by which time it would be too late to do much about it, since my working days as a designer would be past. But a glimmer of the thought was there, and in a few days something happened that boosted the glimmer into a full-fledged idea.

It came at a party. I didn't go to many parties in those days; I was working full time at David Ellies and going to Columbia full time, and there was little time for fun and games. But I went to this party. It was April of 1979. Rosemary, a friend who lived downstairs in my apartment building, was having a small party, and she insisted that I drop by.

At Rosemary's party that night, I met a remarkable young woman who proved to be the catalyst for my three-year experience in the character of an *old* woman. Her name was Barbara Kelly, a makeup artist who worked for NBC Television in New York.

We found ourselves, two strangers, thrown together, so we talked in the way people do in such situations, superficial talk that follows safe, conventional themes: where do you live, what plays have you seen, what kind of work do you do? Somewhere in the flow of all that small talk, when we got around to talking about our respective jobs, the conversation became more serious, because what I was hearing from Barbara was not only that she was a makeup artist, but one whose specialty was the technical, heavily prosthetic makeup involved in preparing actors and actresses to play roles of much older characters.

Somewhere in my head, a light blinked on.

I remembered the first time I had seen a movie in which the main character had "aged" on screen. It had been Dustin Hoffman, playing the part of an Indian chief in *Little Big Man.* Our family had gone together to a drive-in theater to see it, and everyone but me fell asleep in the car. I watched Hoffman turn *old,* right in front of my eyes, and I cried all through the movie.

"Is that the sort of thing you do?" I asked Barbara. It was, she replied.

"You mean you can take someone as young as twenty-five or thirty and make them look *old* so convincingly they could pass for eighty on the street?" "Of course," she told me, "especially if the facial structure and type of body is right for it."

"Look at me," I said. "Look at my face, and tell me if you could make me look *old.*"

"Of course I could. Your face is just round enough; no high cheekbones; plenty of flesh to work with. You would be perfect. I could make you look *very old.*"

After the party that night, I asked Rosemary more about her friend Barbara Kelly. I learned that she came from a family long involved in the entertainment industry and that her father was also a makeup artist. Barbara worked at NBC and did makeup for the "Saturday Night Live" television show, which at that time was a popular hit with its original cast of such stars as John Belushi, Chevy Chase, Dan Akroyd, and Bill Murray.

The NBC show featured skits that depended heavily on prosthetic makeup which dramatically alters an actor's physical appearance. It was a perfect place for a talented young makeup artist to do her apprenticeship. Barbara also did makeup for several Broadway shows. (It is an interesting coincidence, in view of the impact Dustin Hoffman had on me in *Little Big Man*, that she had recently worked with Hoffman. She had applied his makeup for the Broadway hit, *Death of a Salesman*, in which he played the part of a man nearly seventy years of age.)

The more I thought about it, the more obvious it was. If Dustin Hoffman could look *old*, if John Belushi and Angela Lansbury could look *old*—why not Pattie Moore? I remembered what Barbara's answer had been when I asked if she could make me look older.

"I could make you look *very old*," she had promised.

So I decided. And then, quickly, before I could change my mind, I called Rosemary to get Barbara Kelly's telephone number, and I dialed it.

"Barbara, this is Pat Moore. Do you remember me? We met at that party at Rosemary's apartment last Friday night . . . well, Barbara, you told me at the party that you could make me up to pass for a woman of eighty . . ."

# CHAPTER 2

ONCE I DECIDED TO TRY IT, I WANTED TO move in a hurry.

A few days after the party at Rosemary's, my office mail included a notice confirming my plans to attend a conference on aging in Columbus, Ohio, the next week. The conference, sponsored by Ohio State University, would attract experts on aging from across the country—architects, designers, manufacturers, nursing home administrators, all professionals who worked in one way or another in providing for the needs of the elderly.

If anyone in America knows about older people, it would be this gathering of specialists. I knew personally many of the people who would be attending. If Barbara Kelly could actually disguise me as an *old* woman of eighty, might I be able to attend the Columbus conference that way and see if I could fool the experts and the people who knew me, all at the same time? It would be a dramatic test of Barbara's skills and of the whole idea, now growing in my mind, that I might take on the persona of an older person so completely that people would treat me as such. And then, I reasoned, I could begin to learn what it means to be *old.*

If I wanted immediate feedback on the adequacy of the disguise, from the toughest audience imaginable, then the Columbus conference was the place to try it—but what an audacious thing to do! This was not a costume party, after all, this was a serious group of people. I could walk into that conference looking like a refugee from a comedy show and in a moment become the laughingstock of that whole little world of designers and gerontologists. Just thinking about it gave me the shakes. On the other hand . . .

I told Barbara what I wanted to do. "When is this trip?" she asked, "How long do we have?"

"Three days. I leave in three days."

"I think we can do it," she responded, hesitating a moment; "Not the way it should be done—that takes several days. We can do it in three days, but we really have to scamper!"

And scamper we did. The next three days were a blur of activity for Barbara and me. When we paused to think about what we were doing, we felt like co-conspirators, and there developed in those three days a camaraderie that was the basis for the close friendship which we later shared.

Barbara and I bear a striking resemblance; people often think we are sisters. I met her just after my marriage broke up, and she became my close friend and confidante. When we met to begin preparations for the Columbus experiment, we both sensed that the personal chemistry between us was right. It made everything which followed easier.

Barbara explained the makeup procedure for the kind of total facial change which I needed. It required making a plaster cast of the face, then creating customized prosthetic pieces to fit the contours of the face, thereby changing its shape. There was no time for that process before the Columbus conference—that would have to wait—so she did the best she could by using premolded pieces and cutting them to fit.

These pieces would be fitted onto my face, then a layer of flesh-toned latex would be painted over the entire surface, from my hairline to the bottom of my neck, with the lips being the only area of skin not covered. The latex would adhere to the face; the seams would be smoothed out and joined with spirit gum, then the whole area covered with regular facial makeup.

Off Barbara went to a theatrical makeup shop. She bought prefab jowls, crow's feet, bags for under the eyes, and extra skin to put into the neck. She cut them to fit as well as she could. I was an unusually apt subject for prosthetic aging since I have a fleshy face and a chubby nose to start with.

A wig would take care of the hair. We tore into a makeup and costume shop one afternoon, hastily selected a white wig, made the purchase, and dashed out again. It was that kind of operation.

We had no appropriate wardrobe, so we assembled one from whatever we could find around our apartments. I found a pair of canvas shoes I thought might

fit the character, and an old straw purse that had belonged to my mother. We selected a skirt and blouse
from my sister's closet. We added a cane. By bits and
pieces the costume was patched together until we felt
we had a credible version of the garb of a woman in
the seventy-five to eighty-five age range.

In that first experience, my goal was only to *appear*
older, and not necessarily to *feel* older. That would
change later. As I got more deeply into character, I
would seek ways to simulate not just the appearance,
but the vulnerabilities and limitations which older people feel. In the beginning, I simply wanted the disguise
to work well enough that other people would see me
as an *"old* lady," and respond to me according to that
perception.

Even that first time, the transformation was a thor-
ough one. I wrapped my legs with Ace bandages, and
wore support stockings over them. I wore dainty white
gloves to hide my youthful hands. To flatten my chest,
I wore a cinch under my blouse. I'm not a large woman,
but without that treatment my breasts were much
higher than they should have been. Over my white
wig went a pillbox hat with veil. Next I added a pair
of old spectacles with clear glass in the frames.

My teeth were a problem. They were too white and
too regular for most women of eighty. We used a special type of crayon mixed with oil paint, working it
into the teeth, so that they appeared to be stained
and discolored with age. We never solved the problem
of the teeth being too straight (there were few ortho-
dontists around fifty years ago), so I tried to remember
to keep my lips closed as much as possible. I didn't
intend to say much anyway, that first time in character.

To simulate the posture of the role, I tried to coach myself to walk slowly and in a slightly bent-over fashion. This was difficult to do convincingly, and later we would devise an improvement on that approach, but in the beginning I had to fake it. At least I had my cane as a prop and a constant reminder.

My plans were to fly to Columbus on Tuesday morning from New York's LaGuardia Airport. I would need to travel in the old-woman character since I would have no way of getting the makeup done after I arrived. I decided not to tell anyone at the conference what I was doing; I would just arrive unannounced and see what happened.

Would the disguise work? Or would people look at me when I walked into the conference and say, "There's that fool Pat Moore dressed up like an *old* lady"? I didn't know; I wouldn't know until I got there; but it was going to have to be all or nothing. It just didn't seem possible to do this halfway.

On Monday night we had a last run-through of the procedure, Barbara and my sister and I. We did everything but the makeup itself—that would have to wait for the real event. We all agreed that it wasn't perfect, but considering the three-day notice, it was very good.

I was ready to go.

## CHAPTER

# 3

I SLEPT RESTLESSLY THAT NIGHT. THE ALARM clock rang at 4:00 A.M., and by the time I rolled out of bed and plugged in the coffeepot, Barbara was already knocking at the door.

She came in, squinting against the bright light of the makeup lamp which I had just switched on in a corner of the room.

"Coffee?" I asked as she sorted through the supplies which covered the table.

"Please."

I set a mug in front of her and took my place on a stool. She adjusted the lamp, scanned my face critically, and bent toward me for a closer inspection. "Not enough sleep," she grumped, "but that's okay. No problem."

With a sip of coffee, she started to work. By now

my sister Barbie had joined us, and we reacted quietly to Barbara's commands, offering her clips as she pinned my hair into place.

That done, she arranged her makeup and supplies, carefully unwrapping pieces of molded latex, and placing them alongside an assortment of tubes, bottles, and jars on the table.

The mood was somber, almost grim. The run-through the night before had been fun, lots of girlish giggles, like a trio of sorority sisters. Until that morning, it had been an adventure; but in that cold, dark predawn reality, it suddenly sunk in for all of us that this was no lark. This was no joyride. And we said very little.

After my first conversations with Barbara, I had little doubt that the disguise would work, but when she started putting on the makeup, I realized I might have bitten off more than I intended. What I was about to do was professionally risky, and I felt like I was preparing to go into battle.

With my hair pinned neatly in place on top of my head, Barbara carefully applied the preformed pieces to my face, then began the treatment with the latex covering. She would pull my skin out around the natural folds and take the rubbery liquid and spread it over the skin. Then she'd use a hand-held hair dryer to blast it dry. Three coats were usually required to get it right. The technique uses the natural folds, but accentuates the wrinkles and sagging skin. The dried latex forms a mask covering the entire face.

I could feel my nerves tighten as Barbara worked. My sister reached over, touched my knee, and smiled. There was beginning to rise up inside me a thin edge of panic, and she could sense it. "Hey Pattie," she called softly, "You all right?"

I nodded.

Barbara Kelly was moving more quickly now. "Close your eyes."

I obeyed.

"I'm going to dry the latex now," she warned, and the blast of hot air from the dryer hit my face. I jerked back reflexively, then held still, eyes squeezed firmly shut, as she worked.

Next came the powder, a little rouge, then she was finished. "Time for the hair!" she said.

I answered her with a sneeze and opened my eyes. She took the wig from its box and adjusted the curls.

"Hold the front and I'll pull from the back," she directed, and together we stretched the wig into place.

"Use lots of pins, Barbara," I cautioned her. "It's going to be a long day and I don't want this thing to move."

She intently pushed hairpins through the mass of strange hair which capped my head. I yelped as an errant pin stabbed my scalp, and we laughed. It helped break the tension.

"There!" She stood back to appraise her work. "Let's get you dressed."

We wrapped my legs, put on the support stockings, pulled the halter cinch over my chest, then the blouse and skirt. For a moment we couldn't find the shoes, and when we did, I moved too quickly as I sat down to put them on. I began to topple.

"Whoa!" I exclaimed in surprise, grabbing Barbara's arm to try to steady myself as I fell into a chair. "I forgot about the bandages!"

"Put the sweater on," she coached me, as I stood again. "And the gloves." I pulled the last finger into place and smoothed my skirt. I raised my head, turned toward Barbara, and saw her expression change.

"Oh my goodness!" She stopped smiling. "Oh my gosh!" She yelled into the next room, "Barbie, come here, quick, come and look at this!"

Barbie ran in from the next room, took one look at me, and froze stockstill in the doorway. "Pattie Anne Moore, I don't believe it!" she whispered.

We stared at each other until I spoke.

"Barbie? What is it?"

"Look at the mirror," she said, swinging the bedroom door closed.

I turned to see my reflection. I was unprepared for how complete the illusion was, how convincing the total effect. Gazing back at me was an *old* woman. A complete stranger. I put my hand to my face, mesmerized by the sight.

"Barbara," I muttered finally, still not taking my eyes off the *old* woman in the mirror, "What in the world are we doing?"

\*   \*   \*   \*

The first step onto the sidewalk was the hardest. I've never felt so alone. Until now, this was a shared adventure, but from here on, it was going to be just me and the Good Lord.

There weren't many taxis cruising First Avenue that time of morning, and I had to remember that I couldn't rush aggressively into the street to flag down the few that passed. Finally an empty Yellow Cab turned up my block, and I raised the cane to elbow height and got the driver's attention. He jolted to a stop at the curb and opened his door.

New York cabbies see lots of strange things, and in that sense, it wouldn't have mattered much whether my disguise fooled him or not. I would be just one more weirdo in a typical day full of weirdos. But in this case, the cabbie was the first disinterested stranger I faced in the character of the *old* woman, and I was nervous about his reaction. I badly needed him to take me at face value as a woman of eighty years. Headed as I was for Ohio and a conference of professional gerontologists, my confidence needed a boost. If a cabbie had been suspicious of my disguise, I might have abandoned the whole idea right there.

"Let me help you with that, ma'am." He smiled at me and reached for my bag, opening the rear passenger door as I stepped off the curb.

"Thank you," I mumbled.

I worried about my voice. How does an *old* woman sound? I had thought little about it, but now it seemed critical to the character. It was a problem which I eventually would solve, but that day in the taxi, rushing through the early morning traffic to LaGuardia, I decided this was a case in which silence was truly golden. I would say as little as possible, say it as softly as possible, and hope not to give myself away.

We had traveled no more than ten blocks uptown when it became obvious that the cabbie was a talker— or, in this case, a shouter. At the first traffic light, he reached behind him and slid the protective shield fully open. "I HAVEN'T BEEN ON A PLANE IN TWENTY YEARS!" He was shouting at me. "THAT WAS IN THE

SERVICE, AND I ONLY GOT ON A PLANE THEN BECAUSE I HAD TO." He looked over his shoulder at me and smiled broadly.

I nodded and smiled back.

The noise from the city streets was hardly loud at all, certainly not loud enough to require the high decibel assault which he directed at me. "YEAH, I NEVER LIKED THE IDEA OF FLYING," he roared.

It was clear that he was talking loudly for the simple reason that I was *old*. That was it, of course. He thought I was *old*, so he assumed I was somewhat deaf. That was my first sure sign the disguise was working with this stranger. He had no apparent suspicions.

"ARE YOU OFF TO VISIT FAMILY?" he blared.

Part of me wanted to yell at him, "I can hear you, young man, please don't shout!" But I was so pleased at the obvious implications of his exaggerated volume that I hardly minded the roar.

"No. I'm going to a conference in Ohio." I had already decided that, when anyone inquired, I would stick as close to the truth as possible. I would respond as myself. My name was Pat Moore. I lived alone, in New York City. I worked as a designer. I had no children. (It was amazing, over the next three years in disguise, how much that simple biography sufficed to answer people's questions. I had worried about the problem of misrepresenting the truth to people. In fact, it was never a problem. I found that when I told them a few bare facts, they filled in the blanks for themselves.)

"WHAT KIND OF CONFERENCE IS IT?" the cabbie yelled.

"It's focusing on consumer products for the elderly."

"No, thank you. I'm fine."

I was soon seated, strapped in, and on my way to Columbus. As the jet droned on, high above the scattered spring clouds, I reflected on the amazing degree to which people were already reacting to me differently in this character I was playing than they would have responded to the young woman of twenty-six who lived underneath all that latex and support stockings.

I now wore a visible label, and the label was *"OLD,"* and it changed the way people related to me. For some, my wrinkles and stooped body were a signal to offer help, to behave protectively toward me, to give me an edge I wouldn't have been given otherwise. For others, like the man in the seat beside me on that flight, I was something to avoid; he seemed reluctant to engage me in conversation for fear I might drool on his coatsleeve, or go into some sort of senile fit and thrash him with my cane, or have a cardiac arrest right there in the seat next to him.

So he, like many others I would encounter, tried not to notice me at all, though he was an elderly man himself. He buried his head in his newspaper and resisted my gestures toward communication all through the flight. *Old* people are trouble, he seemed to be saying, and I've got enough trouble without getting involved with this *old* lady beside me. I couldn't resist imagining how differently he might respond to me if I had boarded the plane as a fashionably dressed, unmarried career girl of twenty-six.

I had not expected to learn much in the few hours it would take me to travel from my apartment to the conference at Ohio State, but from the moment I stepped to the curb and swung my cane toward that taxi, I began feeling some of what it means to be *old.*

I could sense that it was going to be quite a trip, this journey I was beginning with an *old* lady named Pat Moore. The most important discovery of the morning was that everyone I met, from the cabbie to the skycap to the flight attendants and fellow passengers, looked at me and saw an *old* woman.

But I knew that the ultimate challenge, the acid test, was waiting for me in Columbus. The more I thought about the professional friends and specialists in aging who waited there, the more my anxiety grew. I began to feel that fear again, as I had in my apartment, that feeling that I was going into battle, with no guarantee of the outcome.

The "No Smoking" sign blinked on, and we began our descent toward the Columbus airport.

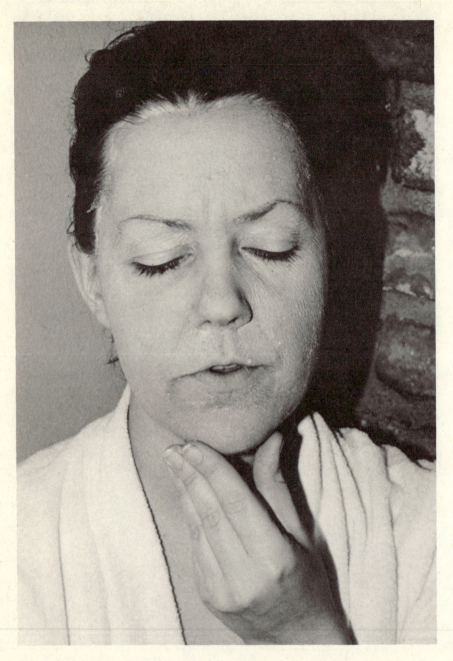

Pat begins the makeup process, slowly building layers of latex on her skin. (Photo by Bruce Byers.)

# CHAPTER

## 4

I WAS TO BE MET AT THE COLUMBUS AIRPORT by a friend, David Smith, who had known me well for a long time. David and I had worked together at the Ellies design firm, and he was also attending the conference.

When I walked off the plane and into the waiting area, I saw Dave standing in the concourse, scanning the stream of passengers as they came toward him. He looked at me briefly as I walked past him, and without hesitation his eyes moved on. I walked back to where he was.

"Hello, David!"

He turned toward me, mild surprise on his face, without a sign of recognition.

I paused a moment longer, thinking that if I gave him a few seconds to look at me closely, it might register on him who I was.

Nothing. He wasn't going to figure it out.

"It's me, Pattie."

His half-smile evaporated. His jaw sagged in surprise. He peered intently at me as if he, or I, or someone were surely demented.

"Pattie? Pattie Moore? What are you doing?" His voice got a bit louder, "Pattie, what on earth are you *do*ing?"

"Relax, Dave. It's okay. I just thought it would be interesting to see how the people at this thing will treat an *old* lady. So I thought this way I could see for myself." I gestured at my clothes, and turned my head from side to side, "So what do you think?"

He appeared to be in shock. "Pattie, are you sure you know what you're doing?"

"I think so."

He looked around us, as if afraid someone might be watching. "Well, let's go," he finally suggested. "We're already late."

And with that he fell right into his appropriate role— that of the conscientious grandson. When the baggage arrived, he took my suitcase in one hand and gently took my arm with the other, guiding me through the exit door. "The car's over here, Grandma," he smiled. "Are you all right?"

"Yes, dear, thank you."

As we drove away, he looked at me again and again, shaking his head.

"I can't believe you're doing this, Pattie. It's incredible. I've always known you were a strange one, but you've never done anything quite this bizarre."

I explained to him how the idea had developed, how strongly I felt the need to know better how older people are treated in all the small, everyday interactions. How could I expect to understand their needs, to help design better products, develop new concepts, without a sharper sense of their daily experience?

By the time we reached the conference site, David was an enthusiastic collaborator in my plan. He let me off at the entrance, parked the car, then rejoined me. We saw from the schedule that the first session had just concluded, and a coffee break was beginning.

We climbed the steps and entered the complex, making our way through a maze of hallways to the designated room.

Dave bent over and whispered, "Okay, Pattie, here we are. Are you ready?"

"Let's go."

The room was full of conferees, meeting, mingling, exchanging introductions over cups of coffee. I took a deep breath and joined the group. Greeting each person I encountered in my path with a nod and a smile, I edged through the crowd.

I saw many people I knew, and maneuvered myself within view of several of them. The reaction was the same in each case: a nod, perhaps a smile, maybe even a "How are you?" but never an indication they recognized me, and never an offer to engage in conversation. After thirty minutes in that room, amid the chatter and hubbub of all those friendly people, no one had attempted to talk to me, none of the little groups had welcomed me to join them.

Clearly, the disguise was working.

On the other hand, it was working so well that I was being treated like an uninvited guest at a family reunion! In that group of specialists, a collection of otherwise gregarious and convivial individuals, an *old* lady of eighty-five was someone to be ignored. She was not the object of hostility or resistance—it was just that she didn't count. She didn't matter much one way or the other.

I had read in my gerontology books about the problem of social "dismissal" of the aging—that is, that they are apt to be ignored, dismissed, or overlooked as if they were part of the furniture or the wallpaper. Now I was getting a taste of it, and I didn't like it. I understood "dismissal" better after half an hour in that room than I ever would by reading about it.

Throughout the conference that day, the pattern persisted. I began to relax about being exposed. I took a seat in the front row of the large conference room, spread my papers and other belongings on the table in front of me, and listened to the speakers just as if I were not in character.

At a break later in the day, I decided to share my secret with another colleague. This was going too well not to let someone else in on it. I recognized Dick Hollerith, a friend who worked for the President's Council for the Handicapped, sitting at a table against a windowed wall.

He was alone, so I approached him.

"Hello, Dick," I said brightly, in my best young voice.

He stared, confused by my familiarity.

"I'm Pat Moore," I offered.

"Pat?" He frowned, then smiled, then laughed aloud. "What are you up to, Pat?"

"I wanted to see how it felt to be *old*," I explained simply, as if it were a quite natural thing to do. "This seemed like the best way."

And when I told him all about it, he approved enthusiastically, and asked if he could tell a mutual friend of ours, the chairman of Ohio State's Design Department. "The possibilities of this are endless, Pat," he beamed.

"I'm just beginning to realize that," I admitted, thinking of how quickly I had become irritated by the way I was dismissed and ignored by all these younger people.

By 3:30 that afternoon, I was beginning to feel claustrophobic under the latex mask, the wig, the whole garb. I had been in character for almost ten hours, and my nerves were getting badly frayed. I kept wanting to take my fingernails and rip my false face off. It was time to get out.

I slipped from the auditorium, left the conference area, and retrieved my luggage from the reception desk, where I had left it that morning. I found a women's lavatory in a different, relatively isolated part of the building. Placing my suitcase on the floor, I removed a change of clothing and an assortment of makeup.

I stood and faced the mirror.

"Bye for now, dear," I whispered to my reflection, and began to remove the hairpins which secured the wig. I pulled the mass of white hair from my head, and felt a wave of relief. The elastic mesh had been very tight, and my head pounded with the surge of fresh circulation. I leaned against the edge of the sink, feeling suddenly faint.

Raising my head, I looked at the face in the mirror. The illusion was shattered; the wrinkles and folds seemed strangely misplaced now.

I gently scratched an edge of the latex, and peeled a small piece of the artificial skin from my forehead. I was surprised at how difficult it was to remove. I pawed through my suitcase for the bottle of lotion which Barbara had given me for the purpose.

Nothing there. Surely, I thought, I haven't forgotten that stuff! Panic set in. I checked again, taking everything out of the bag. Still no luck. I was going to have to get this mess off my skin the best way I could, and quickly, before someone interrupted me midway through my peculiar little metamorphosis.

I used soap, working up a heavy lather, and spread the mixture over the surface of my skin. I scrubbed the soapy mass for several minutes, then finally splashed it clear.

It was only partially successful. My face looked as if it were covered with enormous blisters, a collage of broken and peeling skin and exposed fresh flesh. I repeated the procedure. This time the result was better. And again, until finally only a few stray flecks of latex remained. I laboriously removed these one at a time, scratching them off with my fingernails.

My face was blotched and red and awful-looking, but that could be repaired with my regular makeup. I stepped into a stall and shed my clothes, grunting with relief when the cinch came off my chest, then bending over to unwind the heavy bandages from my legs.

I put on a fresh change of clothes, brushed my hair and pinned it up into a bun, and saw in the mirror that the transition was complete. I was once again twenty-six years of age.

"Welcome back," I said to my reflection.

As I rejoined the conference, I received the ultimate

confirmation that the disguise had been equal to the challenge: friends and acquaintances, among whom I had mingled all day, greeted me warmly and welcomed me to the proceedings. It was as if, having been invisible all day, I could suddenly be seen again. The contrast was dramatic, and I knew right then that I had not talked to that sweet *old* lady in the mirror for the last time.

That night, at dinner with a group of friends who were attending the conference, I told them what I had done, and we discussed the implications of such elaborate role-playing. I was encouraged by their enthusiasm for it; they were insistent that the experience should be repeated, and expanded, and they eagerly shared dozens of ideas of how it might be done.

\* \* \* \*

I awoke the next morning to find my face swollen, the skin burning and itchy and covered with a rash. It was a harbinger of trouble to come—there was obviously much I must learn about the chemicals and creams that had lined and wrinkled my face—but that morning I was so euphoric about the success of my venture that I simply fixed my face as best I could with makeup and thought little more about it.

There was one final, satisfying episode at the Columbus conference which sent me home with an even bigger smile. A group of us were standing in a small circle that morning, talking about one of the papers which had been presented, when a stranger joined our conversation. By then, many people had heard about my character, but apparently this fellow had missed the news.

"Hey! What happened to that *old* woman who was here yesterday?" He was addressing Tom Byerts, a friend of mine who had been at dinner the night before. (The late Tom Byerts, a brilliant architect and gerontologist, was a pioneer in the development of housing for the elderly.) "Has anyone seen her today?"

Everyone smiled, but no one answered, and Tom shot me one of those now-what-do-I-say looks.

"Oh, I'm sure she's probably around here somewhere," he said, and everyone laughed. And with that the gentleman became annoyed, almost indignant. He apparently felt that our attitude toward this *old* lady was unduly cavalier, and he launched into a heated speech.

"Well, I think we should be talking to her, and not just laughing about her being here! We need to be listening to people like her. We need to understand what she can tell us!"

No one had the nerve to stop him, and his tirade continued: "We've got to start incorporating the information the elderly can share with us. That's what our work is all about. Resources like that *old* woman are vital to us!"

He paused momentarily, and Tom turned to me and asked calmly, "Do you know where that *old* lady is, Pattie?"

"Over there," I answered, directing my gaze to the luggage on the floor.

"In here?" he repeated, and unzipped a bag and with a flourish pulled out the white wig. "Oh, *here* she is!"

I thought the stranger would faint.

Barbara Kelly and my sister Barbie were waiting

for a blow-by-blow account of my two-day adventure. After I had shared with them the whole experience, Barbara asked the predictable question.

"Well, what do you say, Pattie, are we going to do it again?"

She needn't have asked. I pulled out a legal pad on which I had scribbled throughout the plane ride home. It was filled with ideas for improving the *Old Pat Moore* character, places she might go, things she might try to do.

"Just think, Barbara," I said, "if we could convince that group of people, with only three days to get ready, what if we really took time to do it right!"

CHAPTER

# 5

I AM NOT AN ACTRESS. MANY PEOPLE WHO hear of my experiences in the character of an *old* woman assume that I must be something of an amateur actress, that I went around the streets of New York and other cities acting like an *old* woman.

It didn't work quite that way. If I looked like an *old* woman, and sounded like an *old* woman, and dressed like an *old* woman, it wasn't necessary for me to actually do anything different from what the Young Pat Moore might have done. The important thing is that when I was in character people *treated me* differently, and it was that treatment which I wished to observe and document.

The type of research in which investigators become a part of the subculture they are studying has been used for many years by sociologists and other scholars.

It is called the "participant-observer" method of gathering information and, though research purists have questioned its validity in some cases, it is generally accepted by the academic community as a valuable technique.

It is obvious that many kinds of human behavior are difficult to study for the simple reason that the behavior itself changes when outsiders arrive to do their research. If a psychologist wishes to analyze the activity of inner-city youth gangs, for example, he is unlikely to get a true picture by hanging around the gang's turf in a three-piece suit with a clipboard in hand. A restaurant reviewer certainly gets a distorted view of the quality of service in a place if the maître d' knows he is a restaurant reviewer.

In each case, the observer gets better information if he observes as a participant, rather than as an outsider looking on. If the maître d' thinks the reviewer is an ordinary customer, or the teen gang thinks the psychologist is a fellow gang member, what each sees and hears will be much more reliable and true-to-life.

It was this inside view of life as a senior citizen which I wanted to get, and it was possible only in the role of participant-observer. The risk of detection and embarrassment which I faced by assuming the character of a woman of eighty years never struck me as being particularly intimidating, especially after I saw that the disguise itself was not likely to be penetrated.

People have spoken to me of my courage in attempting this, and I cannot relate very well to that notion. It never seemed to me such an unnatural thing to do, perhaps because I had done similar things before.

The first time I ever attempted to get information

without full disclosure of who I was came while I was still in college. A housing development in downtown Rochester was experiencing severe problems—a growing crime rate, vandalism, high level of robbery and assault. All these problems had created a serious loss of morale among its law-abiding residents, and they were fleeing the place in droves.

Officials of the housing authority had been unable to solve problems of resident morale, partially because they lacked good information about the attitudes of people in the housing project. One of my professors at RIT knew these officials and suggested that, as an assignment, I try to find out what might reverse the downward trend of morale among the residents and what could be done to make them regard the place as more livable.

So I went to meetings of the residents' committee at the housing project. I arranged to have myself introduced merely as an artist, and the people there saw me as an amateur interior decorator doing a school assignment of some sort. They did not see me as a representative of the housing authority, or as an official of any kind, so they felt free to talk about their problems and their attitudes toward the authorities openly, without the need to strike any postures or go off on quasi-political tangents of any kind. To them, I was just a sweet young white child who was trying to get an assignment finished for an art class.

By listening and observing carefully, I was able to develop a proposal for changes in the physical arrangement of the housing project which resulted in higher morale and a greater sense of ownership by the people. Simple things like providing better exterior lighting, rearranging walkways to correspond with actual needs, and eliminating things like shrubbery islands which had become sources of fear for residents at night— small changes of this type all added up to a big difference.

That was the first time I had done a job under such conditions, but it wasn't the last.

While I was working at Loewy's, part of my work on a particular design project required me to operate as a Sarah Coventry trainee. Sarah Coventry is a company that manufactures various types of jewelry and sells it through a network of independent saleswomen, who sell to other women in their homes, much as Avon or Tupperware distributors do.

Sarah Coventry had grown very rapidly, and its home office realized its saleswomen across the country all used their own makeshift versions of jewelry cases to carry and display their various products. The company wanted a uniform sales kit which would meet the needs of all these women, and Loewy's got the contract to develop one. Being a female designer, I was given the assignment to find out what these women needed, and come up with the design.

The obvious place to start was to go to a meeting in which a Sarah Coventry saleswoman was having a jewelry party for prospective customers, watch her do her thing, and go from there. The Coventry home office arranged it; another Loewy staff member—a man—and I showed up for the jewelry party, at a Long Island home, and were introduced to the saleswoman and her all-female guests as designers from Manhattan who were there to observe.

As any intelligent person might have guessed, we

totally wrecked that poor lady's jewelry party. Nothing is more certain to ruin the ambiance of a women's jewelry party than the presence of a male observer. We made the Sarah Coventry saleswoman so nervous she could barely get through her presentation, and we threw a very large, very cold wet blanket on the entire proceeding. And of course we learned nothing about how typical Sarah Coventry meetings operate in normal circumstances because, by being there, we had rendered the whole evening emphatically *ab*normal.

Obviously a different approach would be necessary. It was decided that I would become a Coventry "trainee," traveling with experienced hostesses to learn the business. Each saleswoman I accompanied took me under her wing and did her sales routine in topnotch form.

I belonged. I wasn't a stranger. As I journeyed in this character, I learned what was needed to design a jewelry and sales kit perfectly suited to the demands of a Coventry representative.

Not only did I not mind this kind of assignment; I actually enjoyed it. I respected these women and what they were doing, and I enjoyed being able to observe them quietly without worrying about the effect my presence might have on their normal *modus operandi*.

Participant-observation became an important tool in my work as a researcher and designer. It was predictable, I suppose, that sooner or later my desire to understand the everyday life of the older American would lead me to a similar approach with them. I had no wish to act like an *old* lady, to pretend to be one in the sense of playing a game or tricking unsuspecting and trusting people. What I did want was to move among them without making them self-conscious. I wanted to be part of their conversation and their fellowship without intruding, without spoiling their natural environment by inserting my youthfulness into it.

It made sense to me, and it still does, to go about it in the way I did. I had always been taught the Golden Rule from the Bible, which says, "Do unto others as you would have them do unto you." What that says to me, in practical terms, is this: "Put yourself in their place. However you would like to be treated if you were *old,* that's how you should treat *old* people."

And how can you know how you would like to be treated, if you've never actually been *old?*

What I did was the next best thing.

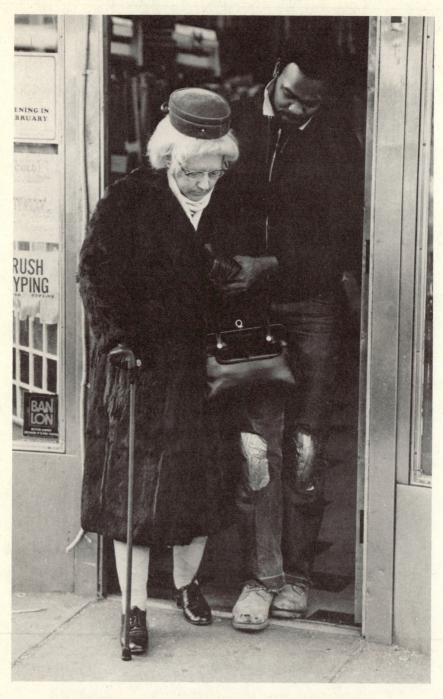

Wealthy character (minimal physical constraints) being assisted by "young" gentleman. (Photo by Bruce Byers, © 1983 by Patricia A. Moore and Associates.)

# CHAPTER

## 6

AS I THOUGHT MORE ABOUT THE FEASIBILITY
of becoming the *Old* Pat Moore on a regular basis, I
was struck by the remarkable combination of favorable
circumstances that made me the right person with the
right idea at the right time. Virtually everything about
my current situation seemed positive.

First, there was Barbara Kelly. She was specially
trained for what we would be doing, she lived nearby,
and was enthusiastic about helping out.

Second, my personal life was such that I was living
alone, had no family with which to mesh schedules,
and was in a period in my life when I needed to stay
busy, to keep my mind off the loneliness that had
threatened to overwhelm me in the months after my
marriage dissolved.

Then there was the advantage of being involved in

graduate studies in gerontology at Columbia University. There I worked closely with a group of highly skilled, dedicated professors, who would be a valuable source of advice and supervision throughout the venture. Though I never attempted to connect my role-playing to the university in any official way, the daily interchange with professors and other graduate students would be an important part of the process.

Fourthly, there was the flexibility and freedom which my job at David Ellies offered. The Ellies office in New York supervised the interior designs of private aircraft all across the country. I was Director of Research and Development, and so long as I did my work, no one was concerned about the hours I kept or the days I didn't come to the office. That would be critical to my plans for the character, since the Ellies job must keep paying the bills during that time.

I thought of all these factors on the plane returning from Columbus, noting them on my trusty yellow legal pad. Another important consideration was the encouragement I had received from my colleagues. Almost without exception, they expressed the view that gathering gerontological information through the "empathic character" of the *old* woman was a good idea.

This opportunity was too good to pass up. I settled on a simple plan: I would refine the disguise as much as possible, then take a day off from work about once a week, leave my apartment, and go to different areas of New York as the *Old* Pat Moore. I would try to place myself in as many different situations as possible, any locale or activity in which women of advanced years might normally be found.

I would walk the streets, sit in parks, shop in stores,

attend Gray Panthers meetings, ride the subways, eat in restaurants and delicatessens. I would try to interact with young people as well as with older ones of all socioeconomic levels, in all sections of town. I would keep my eyes and ears open and see what I could learn. I expected I would learn how people treat the elderly, and I hoped I would learn something about how the elderly themselves feel.

Someone at dinner that night in Columbus had mentioned how valuable it would be for the *Old* Pat Moore to travel to other cities and sections of the country to find out whether what I discovered in New York would also be true elsewhere. At first that sounded a bit ambitious for me, but as I thought about it I realized that, with a little planning, it could be done in conjunction with my job at Ellies. I traveled often to major cities all over the country to work with Ellies clients; and my flexible schedule would allow me to stay an extra day in those cities in character with very little extra expense.

But first the disguise needed some work. Barbara and I started with the wig. We had it styled by a professional stylist, who created a look which matched the age of my character better now than it had off the shelf.

We wanted to simulate many of the sensory conditions which are typical for aging women. We acquired a supply of wax for my ears, the kind of wax used by steelworkers. I would roll it between my hands—it was very soft—and make a plug, which would expand slightly when inserted in the ear. We found an old hearing aid and I wore that in the ear on top of the wax.

We talked with an actor friend who had played *"old"*

characters and found a solution to the problem of my youthful voice. He recommended a technique which he said many actors and actresses use to give the voice a temporary rasping quality which sounds remarkably like that of a very *old* person. Cicely Tyson had used it in *The Autobiography of Miss Jane Pittman*, he said. He taught us to make a thin paste of salt and water, put it in the back of the throat and hold it there for several minutes. After several such treatments, the voice would remain hoarse and raspy for about six hours.

Another problem which we had not anticipated was the clarity of my eyes—they were definitely not the eyes of a woman of eighty-five. We knew we had a problem when my makeup was complete that first morning, and we put the wig on. Only then did the youthfulness of my eyes show; in contrast to the rest of me, they looked like big brown beacons.

I learned that putting little dabs of baby oil in my eyes would fog my vision and irritate my eyes. The look was that of eyes with cataracts, as the baby oil would float on the surface of the eyeball.

We decided to tape my fingers to simulate the lack of movement which people with arthritis must tolerate. We wrapped adhesive tape around them so that I could bend them only with difficulty. And I wore dress gloves to conceal the tape.

Following the principle of not only looking like an older person but also feeling some of their physical limitations, we also devised a more elaborate body wrap to create the body posture of a woman whose frame is bent by the onset of osteoporosis. (We were not creating a fictional character; research shows that more than 50 percent of all women develop some degree of the so-called "dowager's hump" by age seventy-five. This is the slightly hump-backed posture caused by spinal compression fractures due to osteoporosis.)

We developed a body wrap made of cloth that went around my torso and over one shoulder to keep me from standing upright. Sometimes we would put cotton batting under the wrap to simulate a slight hunch. This device placed me in a bent-over posture; I could not stand completely upright if I wished to do so. I was in that wrap several hours at a time, and thinking about it even now makes my back and spine hurt.

It seemed a good idea also to restrain my movement in walking. The idea was the same as with the body wrap: the less I depended on my ability to act, and the more I was physically unable to move freely, the better the disguise and the more fully I could play the empathic character, both at a conscious and a subconscious level. I wanted to be able to concentrate on what was going on around me, not on having to coach myself constantly not to stand upright, or walk too rapidly, or move my fingers too nimbly. So we solved that problem by actually creating the physical limitation whenever possible.

With that in mind, we put small splints of balsa wood behind each knee, kept in place by the Ace bandages. This restricted the flexion of the knee joint. We also pulled a thin elastic tube top—the kind young girls wear as halter tops—up over my hips, which kept me from separating my legs too widely, further reducing the kind of energetic, youthful movement which would be impossible for most women of eighty-five.

I bought an expensive pair of black orthopedic shoes

to replace the canvas ones I had worn. Occasionally I used a walker or a wheelchair, but when I did, it seemed that people responded to me on the basis of my apparent disability rather than on the basis of age alone. For that reason, I seldom used this kind of prop.

Rounding out my wardrobe was easy. To create the effect of women on fixed incomes, I went to the Woolworth store on Thirty-fourth Street and bought a batch of plain cotton housedresses. I got them for $5.99 to $10.99 each and never had a better bargain in my life—size sixteen, I recall, to give me room for the padding underneath. I picked up other things here and there, cotton sweaters and shawls, a few pieces of cheap antique jewelry from St. George's Thrift Shop downtown, and eventually had a complete wardrobe.

The final step in producing the best possible disguise was the creation of a permanent, custom-designed set of prosthetic pieces to go underneath the latex mask on my face. This was the most critical element of the disguise; if the face was not convincing, all the rest would not matter much. We were determined to take the time and spend the money to do it right.

Barbara needed to cast my face to create a mold. It was like being mummified—Edgar Allan Poe should have written a short story about it. I was placed in a special chair—much like a dentist's or barber's chair—and laid back in a prone position. Barbara had all sorts of paraphernalia spread out on a workbench.

She put thick globs of vaseline on my eyelashes and eyebrows, put cotton in my ears and vaseline on them, and pulled a skullcap over my head to protect my hair.

"Relax," she ordered.

(Was she kidding?)

She put two straws into my nose for me to breathe through, then started smearing heavy wet plaster all over my face, ears, mouth, neck, everything right down to my collarbone. After she had finished patting and dabbing the mixture into place, like putting icing on a cake, I lay there breathing through those straws, trying not to succumb to terminal claustrophobia.

When the plaster had dried into a rock-hard mass, it took two people to pull it off my face. Barbara used this as a mold to produce a positive cast of my face, like the death masks one sees in museums. She then used this model of my face to mold prosthetic pieces of lightweight material which custom-fit the specific contours of my own face.

With that done, we felt we had created the best possible disguise for our purposes. It met several important requirements: (1) it made me look very *old* in convincing fashion; (2) it made me feel *old,* in the sense that it created certain limitations which, while in character, I could not escape; (3) the illusion it created did not depend on my ability to act, or to consciously assume any particular posture, tone of voice, or phony characteristic; and (4) it was simple enough that, in time, I could learn to apply it by myself. Though Barbara was available to help me when I was in New York, we realized that she must teach me how to do it alone so I could take the character on the road.

To field-test the refined disguise, I decided to try it out on the most demanding audience I could find. And who, I asked myself, would be most likely to suspect someone disguised as an older person.

Another older person, of course.

That would be my next audience.

# CHAPTER

## 7

THERE WAS NOTHING DRAMATIC ABOUT IT. Looking back, after three years of my journey as the *Old* Pat Moore, that first day of sitting and talking with elderly people seems quite unexceptional. It was something which I later did scores of times.

But that day it was an event of great importance to me; it was another one of those "firsts" I had to accomplish, and like the Columbus trip, it served to build my confidence.

There is a small park in the neighborhood where I live, near the corner of First Avenue and Nineteenth Street. I had noticed a man and woman—they both appeared to be in their seventies—who sat on a bench in that park and talked almost every day. They were obviously not man and wife, since they arrived on the bench separately, coming from different directions.

I had seen these two bench-mates many times, had often nodded and said "hello" as I walked through the park toward my building. The man had two little dogs which usually came with him. On occasion I had stopped to pet the dogs, but I had never engaged him or the woman in a conversation of any length. I decided to try to join them on their park bench one afternoon, to see if I could "pass" as *old* with them.

It was a warm, late spring day when I finally got my garb together, went through the process with Barbara of getting into character, and walked slowly across the little park to approach their bench. I stopped on the sidewalk in front of the bench, greeted them, and asked if they minded if I joined them.

The woman said nothing, obviously deferring to him. Of course they would not mind, he said. It would be their pleasure. With an old-world civility, he welcomed me, and she smiled up at me as if to assure me that she agreed with his response. She seemed shy, blushing like a young girl who is being courted, ever so properly, by the boy next door.

I stayed with them for almost an hour, saying very little, but interacting as naturally as I knew how. He did most of the talking for all three of us, holding court for us two appreciative females. I had worried that even if I had succeeded in *looking old*, I might not *seem old* to these people. As the hour progressed, I was aware that it was working, that I was indeed not sending out invisible vibrations that would tell these senior citizens that I was not one of them.

The other thing which impressed me that day was the generally positive tone of the conversation on the park bench. I would make note of the same thing many times in the next three years; the content and tone of conversation among elder citizens is not gloom and doom and despair, as some might guess it to be.

Many times I have been asked, when people learn of the hundreds of hours I spent in character among older people, "What do they talk about?" I sometimes turn the question back again: "What would you guess they talk about?" And usually the young person asking the question offers that the conversation probably focuses on how the world, and especially the young people, are going to hell in a wicker basket. Many people imagine that older Americans sit around complaining about life in general—the high cost of living, the Social Security check that didn't arrive, how they are ignored by ungrateful relatives, and the rising tide of crime in the streets.

There is a widely held notion that older people sit around playing "Ain't It Awful" with each other all day. That stereotype, like so many others, simply is not an accurate one.

I was forcibly struck that day on the park bench with the bright and optimistic tenor of the talk. That day, as in most such conversations which I observed, I heard older people talk proudly of children and grandchildren, express delighted amazement at the latest developments in science and technology about which they had heard, or share an eagerness to leave something behind for their families.

Older Americans have many concerns about inflation, crime, and loneliness, to be sure, but I learned that they generally whine and complain less, despite more valid reasons to do so, than any other group of people I have ever been around.

It felt good to sit on the park bench with my new friends that day. I almost forgot that, in a sense, I was on trial, and they were the jury. The question of whether or not I would "pass" as being *old* was almost forgotten, so naturally and warmly did they receive me. And, further, the experience confirmed my hopes that by seeming to be one of them, I might indeed learn things about older citizens which I could not discover in a gerontology class.

When my predetermined, self-imposed time limit was up, I hated to leave.

I thanked them for letting me join them, rose stiffly from the bench, and said good-bye. The gentleman was wearing a dress hat, and he tipped it in response.

"Come visit anytime," he offered.

She smiled and nodded that she agreed.

It was perfect.

\* \* \* \*

Over the next three years, I went into character as the *old* woman in 116 cities in fourteen states and two Canadian provinces. I rarely missed a chance, when traveling on business, to add a day or half-day as the *Old* Pat Moore to either end of my professional duties.

Though most of my time in character was spent in New York City, I was eager to learn whether substantial differences exist in the treatment of *old* people between big cities and small towns, the East Coast and the South and the Midwest, or along other demographic lines.

The short answer to what I found is that none of

these factors make much difference. Although older residents have different sets of problems in the big cities than they have in the small towns, the overall quality of life seems little different in either case, and the human dimension—the attitudes and treatment they receive from others—is definitely no different.

Nor did I find a distinctively better attitude toward older people in the Sunbelt cities, or in "retirement towns" with large concentrations of senior citizens. In some of those areas, the younger population has a tendency to take an us-against-them attitude toward the graying neighbors who sometimes appear to be taking over their communities. It has been called "Generation Wars," this friction that develops between the young and the *old* in such areas, and I can personally attest that it can be a real problem.

There is only one variable which in my experience is a reliable predictor of how one might treat his or her aging neighbor, and it is that deeply religious people tend to be more caring and aware of the needs of older people.

There are exceptions, of course, but generally I found that, when it comes to their attitudes toward older people, those who believe in a power greater than themselves are different from those who don't. The church has often been accused of being uninvolved in social issues, but on the issues of aging it is far more sensitive than society in general. The Judeo-Christian sense of the individual as being important in an ultimate reality translates into better treatment of the *old.*

I think it is accurate to say that people who know God care for God's children, no matter what their age.

Wealthy character with friend Bertha Wegis. (Photo © 1983 by Patricia A. Moore and Associates.)

## CHAPTER

# 8

ALMOST EVERY WEEK AFTER THAT FIRST visit in the park, I went into character and lived part of my life as an *old* woman.

The only thing that stopped me was the weather. The artificial skin which I wore had a few weather-related shortcomings. If the temperature got very hot, I was in trouble. Heat would cause the latex to lift off the face; the skin would sweat underneath, and the mask would begin to blister and lose its adhesion to my face. For that reason, plus the fact that my face became very uncomfortable in hot weather, I went into character much less frequently during the muggy "dog days" of July and August.

Cold weather, on the other hand, was excellent for the *Old* Pat Moore. The latex covering hardened and became much more manageable. The system of straps

and cinches which forced my body into its eighty-five year shape were also less uncomfortable during cold weather.

Snow and rain, however, were disastrous for me. If my face got wet, the seams where the latex joined the skin would pull up. This was particularly a problem around my lips. I had to eat and drink carefully, since too much moisture could cause the latex to tear away around the mouth. That meant I couldn't lick my lips, no matter how dry and parched they were.

There were times when the net effect was that I was almost unbearably uncomfortable. Occasionally my skin became so irritated that I could barely control the urge to tear at my face with my fingernails, to rip it off, anything to relieve the discomfort. Fortunately, those occasions were infrequent. Far more often I was able to forget about the makeup and costume almost entirely, and to lose myself mentally in the empathic character.

The longest period in which I was in character without a break was twenty hours, in Boston. Long periods like that one created serious problems for my skin, and at one time those problems threatened to terminate the whole operation.

My face has always been sensitive. I have a variety of unidentified allergies, and since girlhood my face has broken out even with the application of certain skin creams. After the first trip to Columbus, Barbara and I knew we had to deal with the problem or we couldn't continue. We went to see an allergist, and he suggested that I rub hydrocortisone cream into my skin before applying the latex.

This helped, but didn't solve the problems. After

taking my artificial face off, my skin would be swollen and red, and would not return to normal for about twenty-four hours. The latex we used contains a trace of ammonia, which was apparently the culprit. My morning-after condition was uncomfortable, but not life-threatening; so I talked myself through it.

After several months in character, I noticed a small cyst appearing on my forehead. Barbara rushed with me to a dermatologist, who confirmed that the benign growth was probably caused by the chemical battering I was giving my face. He was able to burn the cyst out as a simple office procedure; but before my days in character were over, I had to go back to the dermatologist four times to have such cysts removed.

The constant problems with my skin, capped by the frightening discovery of those facial cysts, were concerns for me as I explored the world of the *Old* Pat Moore, but not even the threat of skin cancer could dim my enthusiasm for what I was doing.

I looked at it, rather philosophically, as a trade-off: no pain, no gain, as the saying goes. I had voluntarily turned my face into a "toxic dump" with all those chemicals. I should have expected problems galore, and I got them.

The payoffs, on the other hand, were unexpectedly meaningful. I began this whole experiment with the hope that I would be better able to serve the elderly community. I was seeking to learn better how to help *them,* and instead, in many small interactions with older people, I could see that it was they who were helping me.

The first, most moving encounter of this type came in my very first month in character. It was June of

1979. It was a day, I suspect, which I'll never be able to forget because it was the day that the papers arrived in the morning mail, officially and irrevocably closing the door on the marriage which I had thought would last forever.

I hoped that I had used up my quota of pain, that seeing the official documents in black and white would not shake me. But when I opened the envelope and looked at the words, so coldly pronouncing the end of my marriage, the emotional force of it struck again. I was sick. I was numb.

Fortunately, as it turned out, I was in character at the time. I didn't have the energy to go through the laborious process of changing—it didn't matter much anyway, at the moment. Nothing seemed to matter much right then.

I left the apartment and made my way along the city sidewalks, replaying all the joy and hurt, the promise and betrayal that every broken marriage contains. I found myself headed for Washington Square Park, a large park near New York University which I knew well. I walked under the massive memorial arch, made my way to a bench in the shade, and sat down heavily, alone.

On such a fair June day, people filled the park: NYU students playing frisbee; kids bopping by on roller skates, their headphones providing the beat; couples walking arm in arm. On any other day, it would have been a lovely scene, but today it added to the bleakness of my heart. I couldn't forget that back home in my apartment, lying on a tabletop, was that legal document. It would not go away. My marriage was over.

Even in my disguise, there was no place to hide,

no way to escape. So I sat, looking like an *old* woman, but feeling very much like a discarded young woman, numb and crying in Washington Square Park, feeling isolated and totally alone.

I closed my eyes against the pain and the memories. I don't know how long I sat there that way.

"Is there anything I can do to help, dear?" The voice was soft, barely audible.

I opened my eyes and through my tears saw an *old* woman standing in front of me. She was smiling, as if to signal friendliness, but behind the smile was obvious concern.

Before I could respond, she asked, "Would I be intruding if I joined you?"

I shook my head, "No, please, sit down." And I pushed my cane and purse aside to make a place for her.

After sitting, she paused, looking at me, then turned to look ahead, in the direction I was staring. She must have sensed I was not going to respond further, so she sat quietly for a moment, then without turning back in my direction, spoke quietly: "Are you ill, dear? Are you sure there is nothing I can do to help?"

"No, really. I'm fine." It was a half-hearted denial, so empty I feared it might sound as if I resented her intrusion. Somehow I didn't want her to leave. I quickly added, in a voice I hoped was less morose and broken, "I guess I'm just feeling a bit blue."

She smiled at me, and I smiled back.

"Oh, well, you needn't be embarrassed by that," she said, turning toward the sound of a young boy laughing, as he ran past us. "I know how those days are."

Looking at me again, she asked, "Would it help to talk?"

For one of the few times in the two-hundred-plus occasions that I was in character, I considered revealing myself, telling her that I was not *old,* but very young, telling her all about it, all about everything. As an industrial designer and gerontological researcher, I knew I should stay in character; but as a lonely young woman, I was tempted to abandon the whole thing right then and there, so badly did I need the comfort and support I felt coming from this stranger, this kind woman.

"Yes," I said. "I've been sitting here, thinking about my marriage." I paused and took a deep breath before continuing. "It ended in an annulment." My voice wavered and trailed off.

"How long were you together?"

"Not very long. About eight years, all together."

"You loved him very much?" She was making a statement, more than asking a question.

I turned to her and nodded, dabbing at my eyes with a little cotton handkerchief I carried.

She placed her hand on mine.

"I never married. I was in love once, but he died, in the war," she paused and sighed. "I never found anyone like him."

She turned away.

We both watched the children at their play.

Calm had replaced my misery, and we sat and chatted almost until dusk.

I never saw the woman again, which was not unusual, but the time she spent with me on the bench in Washington Square Park provided an emotional healing that was nowhere else available. It was a loving, unconditional concern, the kind that the *Young* Pat Moore needed. That kind of exchange is much more common between older people, I believe, than between people of ages representing less life experience.

I don't know who she was. She might have been an angel.

# CHAPTER
# 9

THERE WOULD BE OTHER SUCH TIMES WHEN older people would cheer and encourage me, never guessing I was not the person I appeared to be.

I was repeatedly impressed by the network of mutual support which I found among the elderly people whom I met. There was a comradeship among them which I do not see as frequently in the younger community. It is as if older people understand that they operate under certain disadvantages in this society and that it is important that they stick together for the common good. They seem more likely to sense one another's needs, and more willing to reach out to help, than do people in the general population.

When I was in character, I became one of them. They took me at face value and immediately accepted me into their circle of supportive companionship. It is not stretching the point to say that, during those three years from 1979 to 1981, it was often easier for me to find a community of support when I was in character than when I was not.

As a young woman I had friends, of course, and their interest in me was real and reliable. But those young friends were busy; they had careers and families, sports to play and things to do. It could sometimes be difficult for me, as it is for other young people like me, to find someone with time to simply sit and talk and be together, at the time I needed it.

The *Old* Pat Moore rarely had that problem. I could get into character, find a group of senior citizens somewhere, and almost always count on being welcomed among them. I didn't have to say much, or explain myself to them. I was just there, another aging person who wished not to be alone, and they always had time for me. And when I did choose to talk about myself, to disclose my fears or my contentments, they were always interested and concerned.

Younger people often think and talk of the disadvantages of being *old,* but there are advantages, too, and this is one of them. The accumulation of time can help us prioritize our lives. When we pass threescore and ten, only then will some people find what is really important in their lives and discover the joy of taking time for one another.

The biggest problems in the lives of older citizens— other than the general deterioration of their bodies— arise when they interact with younger people. The young are often badly informed about what older people are like, and stereotypes of the elderly abound. Like stereotypes of any kind, they are often inaccurate or downright abusive.

Too many younger Americans think of their older counterparts as uniformly deaf, forgetful, arthritic, cranky, and hard to deal with. Many younger sales-clerks, bank tellers, and waitresses see someone over seventy as a customer who is likely to be troublesome, creating difficulty of some sort.

As with most stereotypes, there is just enough truth to keep the larger fiction alive. If younger people expect elder citizens to fit this negative pattern, they avoid them if they can, give bad service, find ways to ignore them entirely, or treat them with condescension and dismissal. That attitude inevitably increases the likelihood that the older person will behave impatiently, and the spiral of self-fulfilling prophecy is complete. It is a fundamental truth that people tend to act the way they are expected to act. If younger Americans expect senior citizens to act like Clara Peller in the infamous Wendy's commercial ("Where's the beef?"), their encounters with the elderly are likely to be unpleasant ones.

When I did my grocery shopping while in character, I learned quickly that the *Old* Pat Moore behaved—and was treated differently—from the Young Pat Moore. When I was eighty-five, people were more likely to jockey ahead of me in the checkout line. And, even more interesting, I found that when it happened, I didn't say anything to the offender, as I certainly would at age twenty-seven. It seemed somehow, even to me, that it was okay for them to do this to the *Old* Pat Moore, since they were undoubtedly busier than I was anyway. And further, *they* apparently thought it was okay, too! After all, little *old* ladies have plenty of time, don't they?

And then when I did get to the checkout counter,

the clerk might start yelling, assuming I was deaf, or become immediately testy, assuming I would take a long time to get my money out, or would ask to have the price repeated, or somehow become confused about the transaction.

What it all added up to was that people feared I would be trouble, so they tried to have as little to do with me as possible. And the amazing thing is that I began almost to believe it myself! Psychologists call it "identification with the aggressor." Even though I wasn't genuinely *old,* I became so intimidated by the attitudes of others, by the fear that they would become exasperated with me, that I absorbed some of their tacitly negative judgment about people of my age.

It was as if, unconsciously, I was saying, in reaction to being ignored and avoided, "You're right. I'm just a lot of trouble. I'm really not as valuable as all these other people, so I'll just get out of your way as soon as possible so you won't be angry with me."

I think perhaps the worst thing about aging may be the overwhelming sense that everything around you is letting you know that you are not terribly important any more. Walking along a crowded sidewalk, someone bumps into you and, unless you are knocked literally sprawling, keeps going, as if to say you don't count anymore. As the Young Pat Moore, I had a much better chance of getting an apology or an inquiry about whether I was hurt, or at least a civil exchange of some sort.

Obviously, there are many individual exceptions to this, but the general pattern holds up in all types of situations. As a woman of eighty-five, I might board a city bus one day, and the driver would get out of his seat to help me; the next day, a different bus driver treats me like a crochety *old* bag who is ruining his day by riding his bus. But as a woman of twenty-seven or twenty-eight, I definitely met far more of the good guys and far fewer bad ones than when I was in character.

Was the shabby treatment I so often received as *Old* Pat Moore a reaction to the fact that I was *old*, or when in character did I just happen to encounter merchants who treated everyone brusquely, regardless of age? I wondered about that, and on several occasions I went twice to the same establishments and engaged in the same transactions with the same personnel—once as the younger and once as the older character. In virtually all these comparisons, the people I encountered showed a more positive attitude toward the younger me. Sometimes it was subtle, but the difference was almost always there, and it always worked against the woman of eighty-five.

Typical of these comparisons was a man who operated a stationery store in Manhattan. He was one of those individuals who appear to become instantly irritated by the presence of an *old* man or woman. I entered his store one day to buy a ribbon for my typewriter. I was in character, but I honestly did need the ribbon, and I didn't go there with the intention of returning later in younger garb.

I began looking for what I needed, patiently, without asking for any help, and could not find it. He stayed at the cash register for several minutes without greeting me or offering to help. It was a small shop, and I was the only customer there at the time.

In resignation, he finally approached me.

"Do you need something?" he barked.

"A ribbon for my typewriter," I replied hopefully.

Stepping behind the counter, he asked, "What kind?"

"A black one," I said with a smile. He was so terse that I wondered if I had done something to upset him.

"No, no, no! What kind of typewriter do you have?" By now he made no attempt to hide his irritation; he was addressing me as if I were a half-witted child in a candy store.

"Oh, pardon me. I understand what you mean now," I apologized as sincerely as possible. "I can never remember the name of it. Could you name what you have and I'll know it?"

He sighed in response: "Smith-Corona, IBM Selectric, Olivetti, Adler . . ."

"That's it," I interrupted. "Adler. I can never remember that. I should write it down!"

Without speaking, he left to get the ribbon, returned to the cash register, and began to ring up the sale.

"Three dollars and twenty-four cents, with tax," he stated abruptly.

I began to fumble with the latch on my handbag. It was difficult to open, even without gloves and arthritis. For my older self, it was a struggle.

As I wrestled with the change-purse, he heaved such an exasperated sigh that I felt a need to apologize for the delay.

"Darn thing always gives me trouble!"

No response but the same dull glare.

Having successfully opened the purse, I gave him a five-dollar bill.

Without speaking, he placed the change in my hand and put my purchase into a paper bag.

78

I waited for a moment to see if he intended to hand me the package or address me further. He did neither. Instead, he left the counter, went to the far side of the store, and began busily readjusting the merchandise on a shelf. I picked up the paper sack from the counter and left.

Exactly what transpired in that dreary exchange between the proprietor and the *old* woman? Did it have anything at all to do with an attitude that the *old* are not as important, or not as enjoyable to interact with? Or perhaps it had nothing to do with age; maybe he was just a jerk. Maybe he was rude to everybody.

To test that proposition, I returned to the stationery shop the very next day, hoping to find the same man behind the counter. He was there, and once again he was alone.

I was my younger self now. Sandy-blonde hair curled and falling on my shoulders, sunglasses and sandals. I looked like many other young women from the neighborhood areas around Greenwich Village. I was even wearing the same dress I had worn the day before, but my back wasn't padded to convey a slight hunch, my legs weren't covered by layers of elastic bandages, and the wrinkles and bags were gone from my face.

He looked up immediately as I entered, and gave me his best smile. "Yes, miss? May I help you?" he chirped.

Somehow, I wasn't surprised.

"A ribbon for my typewriter." I said being careful to repeat the previous day's request.

"And what kind would you like, miss?"

"A black one," I answered simply.

"Oh, no!" he laughed, "I mean what kind of typewriter do you have? They're all different, you know!"

"Oh, now I understand," I returned his smile. "I never remember. Could you name what you have and I'll know it?"

"Sure thing," he replied eagerly. "Let's see, I can help you with a IBM Selectric, a Smith-Corona, a Brother, or there's an Olivetti, an Adler . . ."

"That's it!" I exclaimed, just like before. "I can never remember that. I should write it down."

"Oh, lots of people have that problem," he reassured me. "But as long as you know it when you hear it, you're all right."

He was chuckling pleasantly as he placed the ribbon on the counter and pushed the cash register keys.

"Are you sure you don't need anything else with that, now?"

"No, thank you."

"That'll be three dollars and twenty-four cents with the tax," he said politely.

I placed my handbag on the counter. Fumbling with the latch, I repeated my performance from the day before.

"Darn thing always gives me trouble."

"Well, better for it to be nice and tight and take a little longer to open, than to make it easy for the muggers and the pick-pockets," he bantered.

I handed him a five-dollar bill and waited for the change. He counted it out carefully, "That's four and one makes five! Now we'll get you a bag here and you're all set."

He was so nice. I had to fight the urge to scream. Without a word I turned away from the counter and headed toward the door. He scurried behind me.

"Let me get that door for you," he offered, "it sticks sometimes."

"Yeah, I know," I mumbled, and walked out the door.

Does that incident have serious meaning? Not if everyone, like me, could shed the skin and persona of the *old* woman and (*presto!*) become young again. If that were the case, we could laugh it off and poke a little fun at the shopowner, like watching an old rerun of a "Candid Camera" show.

But to the millions of men and women who cannot turn back the clock as I could, it is a too-familiar pattern, and it is not funny at all. Take that incident and multiply it several times every day, and it adds up to one segment of our society telling another segment that they are not worth much any more, that they are unwanted, that they are unimportant.

Middle income character with serious physical constraints.
(Photo by Bruce Byers, © 1983 by Patricia A. Moore and
Associates.)

# CHAPTER

## 10

WHY DO DIFFERENT PEOPLE HAVE SUCH contrasting attitudes toward the senior citizens they meet?

It is a question I am asked often. Apart from the obvious fact that people have different attitudes about all manner of things, are there any identifiable reasons that one person is accepting of older people, and comfortable with them, while another is not?

I am not a psychologist or psychiatrist. If I were, I might be reluctant to try to answer the question for fear that my answer might be too much an oversimplification. I do understand that there are more elaborate reasons buried deep in the psyche of all of us than I will ever understand, but with due respect and apologies to the specialists, I have an opinion that seems worth sharing.

We tend to enjoy being around older people, and place greater value on them, according to two important variables: (1) the quality of the experiences we had with older people as we were growing up, first forming our attitudes and emotional associations, and (2) the degree of comfort which we feel about the prospects of our own aging.

Not only have I always enjoyed the company of older people, but it seems that older people sense it about me. I am the person who always gets picked by older people who need help. I can be standing in line outside a theater with fifty other people, and it seems as if every dear older lady who needs change for a dollar to make a phone call always comes straight to me. It is as if *old* people have radar; when they see me, it locks in, and though I am a stranger they sense they have a friend.

I grew up surrounded by older people. The neighborhood was full of them in the part of Buffalo I knew as a child. I didn't grow up in one of those suburbs where every homeowner is between the age of thirty and forty-five, and the kids get a glimpse of elderly people only when a grandparent occasionally comes to visit. Mine was an old-fashioned neighborhood with a mix of all ages: young families, retired couples on pensions, middle-aged men and women with grown children, widows well into their seventies and eighties. We had it all there, and consequently older people were not just something I saw on television or on city streets; they were my friends and my playmates.

It was a conservative, hard-working middle American neighborhood; we all looked out for each other up and down Moeller Street. I always felt welcome in the homes of the elderly people on our block. There was Mrs. Atkins, the dearest woman in the world, who would invite me to her house, where she would tell me and my sisters stories, and comb our hair in strange styles we had never seen before.

Mrs. Atkins scolded us when we deserved it, but we always knew she loved us as the grandchildren she never had. When I first learned to write, I wrote my name on the lowest shingle on the side of Mrs. Atkin's house. When she had the house repainted years later, my scribbled signature was still there; and she wouldn't let the workers paint over that one shingle!

Mrs. Brenner was another favorite neighbor of all us Moore children. (I have two sisters, Colleen and Barbie, both younger than I.) I liked to stop at her house on my way home from school. She would meet me at the door, and hold my hand as we walked into her kitchen. I would take my place at the table while she went to the refrigerator, removed a loaf of bread from the vegetable bin (that's right—bread in the vegetable bin), and pulled out a jar of grape jelly.

She would smear the jelly on a piece of bread, then cut the bread up into little squares which she called "baby sandwiches," custom-made for my benefit. Then she would pour me a glass of milk, place the plate of bite-sized snacks in front of me, and we would talk while I ate. I ate slowly, because when I was finished, it would be time to go home.

I only knew two of my grandparents; my Grandfather Moore died several years before I was born. And my mother's mother—my Grandmother Leising—died when I was a young girl.

The other two grandparents were important people

in my life, though, and I am convinced that the positive experiences I had with them predisposed me to the acceptance and love of older people which I have always felt.

We all lived in the same house with our Grandmother Moore through most of my childhood. We lived in one of those double-decker row houses built for two families. Grandmother Moore and my father's sisters lived on the second floor, and we lived below. Since my mother taught school, I spent more time with Grandmother Moore than with Mother during certain periods. We would visit her every afternoon, and after dinner each night would march back upstairs to "Grandma's house" to watch television, with my best memories being such shows as "Rawhide," "Sergeant Bilko," and "Jackie Gleason."

Grandma died during my first month in college. I was sitting in the student lounge, talking with friends, when the call came. I remember my mother's voice telling me that my grandmother was dead, and after that I don't recall any more of the conversation. It was an emotional bodyblow, my first experience with deep, debilitating grief, and it was a long time before I could remember her without crying.

But the grandparent who most profoundly influenced me over the years has been my Grandfather Leising. We have all called him "Dutch" as long as I can remember. Dutch is now ninety-four years of age and still vigorous though he is wheelchair-bound and has failing eyesight.

Dutch has always been the center and focus of our household, anytime he is with us. When I was growing up, he had a favorite chair in our living room, and no one ever sat in Dutch's chair. It was in clear view of the television set, so he could watch his beloved New York Yankees; and at Christmas time it faced the Christmas tree, so he could preside more completely over the family holiday.

What made Dutch a truly exceptional grandparent were his Canadian summers with all the grandkids. What he did with us was so heroic that it must qualify him for some kind of Grandfathers' Hall of Fame, though we kids typically took it for granted in those days.

Dutch had a small, rustic cabin in the woods about one hundred miles north of Toronto, outside of Peterborough, Ontario. The cabin is near the Trent River and a muskie fishing lake called Rice Lake. Each summer for many years, Dutch took all his grandchildren to that cabin for the entire summer—just Dutch and twelve to fifteen kids up in the middle of nowhere for two months.

The big cabin had a single open room with thin partition walls and drapes to separate the space into roomlike stalls for sleeping. Dutch did all the cooking; we were responsible for other chores, the boys chopping wood for the stove and the girls bringing water in pails from a nearby well.

I first spent the summer at Dutch's cabin at the age of seven and never missed a summer until my senior year in high school. I don't know what other kids my age were doing in the summertime during those years, but I was always up in Canada with Dutch. Even after I became a teenager, it never occurred to me not to go.

Dutch was the first person up each day. He got up

by the early morning light, just after daybreak, and slipped quietly out to the front steps of the cabin. The way the cabin is situated in a clearing in the woods, the early morning sun bathed the front stoop when it rose. I enjoyed slipping out of the cabin to sit with Dutch; I would find him there early every morning, in the quiet. I would sit next to him and hug his knee and neither of us talked much.

His routine never varied. When the rest of the kids would begin to stir, he would push his baseball cap back on his head and say to me, "Well, kiddo, how about some toast?" With that we went into the kitchen and he would make breakfast on that wood-burning stove.

We spent the day swimming and fishing in the lake. The nearest mailbox was at a marina, two miles away down a dirt road. The big event was to walk to the marina and get a popsicle, then sit on a big rock by the side of the road and talk and wait for the mail. Dutch never went very far from the cabin, and we kids gravitated around it and him all day.

When sun fell, activity at the cabin on Rice Lake slowed considerably. Dutch cooked dinner, usually the fish we caught that day, with potato pancakes. After the dishes were clean, there was nothing much to do. We talked or played cards for a while; then everyone went to bed early.

To me, Dutch was always the personification of the loving, nurturing older person. He was already almost seventy when I went to Canada with him for the first summer.

It would be difficult for a little girl with that kind of grandfather to grow up afraid of *old* people.

Summer in Canada—Dutch and Magoo in Hastings, Ontario.

CHAPTER

# 11

AFTER MY INITIAL EXPERIENCES IN CHAR-
acter in the spring of 1979, I became gradually more
adventuresome. I was living two lives; in one of them
I was a designer and graduate student, and in the other
I was an *"old"* woman.

I tried to keep the two roles as separate as possible.
On my *"young"* days, the routine was well established.
The David Ellies office was at the corner of Thirty-
ninth Street and Lexington Avenue, about twenty-five
blocks from my apartment. I would be at the office
by 7:00 A.M., work through lunch until 1:00 or 2:00
P.M., then take the subway uptown to Columbia University. My classes began at 4:00 P.M. during most se-
mesters, and I got home late at night. As a full-time
graduate student, there was plenty of studying to do,
and I had to do it late at night.

On my *"old"* days, anything might happen. I usually

left the apartment early and made a day of it, if I spent the day in New York.

As much as I appreciated the salary I earned at traditional design firms, the work itself was not very satisfying. It took me to interesting places and put me in touch with important people, but it had little relevance to my own particular design interest—that of creating better products and environments for consumers throughout their life span. Basically, I was spending my time designing gold-plated faucets for some rich Arab's jet, and though I was paid very well for doing it, it neither stimulated nor fulfilled me.

So while I worked hard to earn my keep, I dreamed of a day when I could bring my energies and concerns as a designer fully to bear on the needs of aging citizens. Doing that, and doing it my way, would require me to run my own design firm, and that was the dream I nurtured through those years.

My studies at Columbia, on the other hand, were specifically related to what I was doing as the *Old* Pat Moore, and provided balance to the perspective I was getting on the street. Dr. Ruth Bennett, who is Deputy Director of the Center for Geriatrics and Gerontology at Columbia, was particularly supportive. She ran interference for me at the university, explaining my rather offbeat brand of research to colleagues accustomed to more conventional approaches.

Though I began with a focus on design problems for the aging consumer, my interest shifted to a greater emphasis on their interactional problems and needs. I began to see that there were more than just design issues at stake. In a sense, I started the project as a designer, and came to function more as a sociologist.

A potential problem was that I was not trained as

a sociologist; I did not have a Ph.D. in any area of behavioral science, and I respected those who did, so I was somewhat reluctant to press my views about *old* people on them. On the other hand, I had been places they had never been, seen things they had not seen, and I became confident that my insights were valid and useful.

There was much debate in academic circles at that time about the advisability of participant-observer research, in which the subjects are, in a sense, fooled by the researcher. As I heard the issue argued at Columbia, I grew concerned about how my work would be received by the academic community. Dr. Bennett, sensing my need for affirmation of my approach by the professional research community, arranged for me to deal in a conclusive way with that concern.

In October of 1979, the PRIM&R organization (Public Responsibility in Medicine and Research) was sponsoring a conference in Boston to examine issues involved in the use of human research subjects in behavioral science. Dr. Bennett arranged for me to attend the conference in character, in order to assess professional reactions to my use of the disguise.

In preparation for the Boston meeting, I made contact with Dr. Stanley Milgram, of the City University of New York, to seek his advice. Dr. Milgram is one of America's best-known psychologists; he conducted a famous set of experiments at Yale in which he demonstrated the willingness of some individuals to administer painful electric shocks to others at the command of an authority figure.

When I told Dr. Milgram of my research, he agreed to meet me in Boston and assess my empathic character. "It's quite an extraordinary model," he observed. "If you're willing, I'd like you to appear as the *old* woman on the first day of the conference. On the second day, I will chair a workshop on the role of deception in research. I'd like you to attend. We'll discuss your role-playing at that time."

*Good grief!* I thought, *What am I getting into this time?* I answered hesitantly, "Okay, sure, Dr. Milgram, I'll be there."

That Boston conference was perhaps the most stressful occasion I experienced in character, but I felt it was something that had to be done. I did not want my work to be a mere stunt; I wanted it to be taken seriously, especially by those professionals in a position to make use of what I was learning to change the way America treats its older citizens.

In the six months since my experiment began, I had become more and more committed to it. By October of '79 I was making a major sacrifice of time and money to be on the street as the *"old"* lady; I was pushing myself to keep the job, the schoolwork, and the character going all at once, and I wanted it to count for something. To accomplish that, I knew I must submit my whole approach to the analysis and criticism of this elite academic group. They would be tough critics, but their approval was imperative.

By the time I got to my Boston hotel room, I was a nervous wreck. I had been in character almost five hours, and I was exhausted, as much from anxiety as from lack of sleep. I felt like a little girl being sent to the principal's office to be scolded for improper behavior. How would I respond if the feedback from this group was negative? What if they thought my work failed to meet the ethical standards which were so sacred to them and so vital to research involving human participants?

I couldn't afford to think about it.

I was more self-conscious that first day at the Boston conference than at any time since the original trip to Columbus. I sat through the sessions all day without relaxing, my antennae attuned to the slightest hint that anyone might see through my disguise. *If ever there was a time to be convincing,* I kept telling myself, *it is now.*

The next day, I appeared at the Milgram workshop as my young self. I was introduced, and the surprise of the audience confirmed that yesterday's disguise had been as convincing as always. After a few introductory comments, Dr. Milgram came right to the point: "Ms. Moore is doing some fascinating research which examines the issue of aging in our society. Pat was an *old* woman yesterday; perhaps some of you remember seeing her? She is here so that we might use her work as a case in point, and examine the ethics involved in her deception."

The room filled with whispers, and it seemed that every eye was on me. I felt like the main attraction at an inquisition.

And then the serious debate began.

The arguments and counterarguments flew across the room in the hour which followed. In the best tradition of spirited academic dispute, the pros and cons of my work were batted back and forth. I felt like the little white ball in a high-speed ping-pong game.

"If one of the goals of sociology is to gain an accurate understanding of an individual," someone offered, "what better way than to *be* that individual?"

"But what are her qualifications for such work? She is a designer, not a sociologist!"

"That doesn't matter, for heaven's sake!"

"Credentials matter a great deal . . ."

"But they must be weighed against the value of the work . . ."

"It's deception . . ."

"Society accepts the desirability of illusions. All illusions are not deceptive . . ."

"It's entrapment . . ."

"Any research using human subjects takes advantage of those subjects. It can't be avoided . . ."

"It's unethical to create a situation that doesn't really exist in the field . . ."

"Of course it really exists! Don't be naive. She's only documenting what we all know is out there . . ."

"She's pretending to be *old* . . ."

"She's not entrapping. She is not announcing that she is *old*. People are reacting to what they perceive . . ."

And so the discussion went. Uncomfortable as I was to be the object of all this debate, and fearful as I was that the group's verdict may be that I should not continue, I must admit that the points raised, on both sides of the question, were compelling and thought-provoking. The debate gave me an appreciation for the gravity of what I was doing that I didn't have before.

When it was over, the consensus was an emphatic affirmation of the legitimacy and value of my use of the empathic character. I was so relieved, I almost cried.

Dr. Milgram summed it up: "Ms. Moore's work is an extension of theatrical technology for investigative purposes. Her role-playing as the *old* woman meets the definition of participant-observation and is therefore a valid research application."

The blessing of the group that day was accompanied by a warning: "You are representing a person who does not exist as she appears. You must exercise caution at all times. There are people's feelings involved, people who will seize this opportunity to have a new friend. To find that the person they see is only a facade could be emotionally very disruptive."

When the meeting was adjourned, I was surrounded by people from the audience who waited to congratulate me, encourage me, ask more questions about my work, and exchange business cards in promise of future contact. It was a circle of smiling, laughing, supportive people, and I felt like hugging and kissing every one of them.

I soaked up their good wishes, and I took their warnings to heart. I was enormously reinforced in what I was doing and at the same time sobered by the concerns they had raised. I was buoyed by their support and excited about returning to New York and getting on with the project, armed now with the confidence that my findings would have the respect and scrutiny of serious behavioral scientists.

# CHAPTER

## 12

I WAS SO HIGH WHEN I LEFT BOSTON THAT I barely needed the Eastern Airlines shuttle flight to get me back to LaGuardia.

The next year was a fruitful time for the little *old* lady named Pat Moore. I saw and experienced many things; some of them angered and frustrated me. I was not accustomed to the limitations and abuses suffered by the very *old*. I had jumped into the role of an *old* person "cold turkey," with no period of gradual acclimation, and sometimes I could barely keep from ripping my wig off and giving someone a very unladylike piece of my mind.

A few times my Irish blood got the best of me, and I unloaded on someone—but never, I hasten to say, on anyone who did not richly deserve it. Once in Florida I went into a drugstore to buy a bottle of medicine for my ailing stomach. I was in character, and the druggist ignored me from the moment I entered. I had to ask for help, and he acted as if it were a big chore merely to get me the bottle from the shelf. It was a hot day, and I was in no mood to be jerked around.

I went back the next day as the *Young* Pat Moore and this fellow, like the man in the stationery shop, was totally different. I asked for the same product and got spontaneous and cheerful assistance. It was a bit too much that day, so I called his hand on it. He probably never has figured out who I was or what I was talking about.

Another time I temporarily lost my senior-citizen cool and whacked a man over the head with my cane. I was hobbling slowly down the street in downtown Pittsburgh, when a young man rushed by me, bumping me hard. I felt he could have avoided it, or at least acknowledged it. He never said "boo" or "excuse me" or anything else. I just turned around, bopped him over the head with my cane, and walked sweetly on my way. I suppose I got out of character, maybe just a bit.

I should have done it more often.

Whenever I made a purchase in a retail store, I was reminded of the difficulty *old* people have in distinguishing among the various coins and bills. As we age, our eye muscles weaken, and the lenses yellow and become opaque. The result is an eye that no longer sees objects clearly, confuses colors, and cannot function as well in low light conditions. What we were able to read easily as teenagers becomes much more difficult to see under the same level of light, when we pass the age of sixty.

Certain color combinations, for example, make it almost impossible to read instructions for appliances or the contents of a package, or prices on labels in a shopping situation. When dealing with money, that difficulty in seeing translates to paying a vendor with a ten-dollar bill when only a dollar is required, and facing the chance of not receiving the correct change. We don't like to admit it, but the number of unscrupulous people who prey on the elderly is not limited to muggers and flim-flam artists.

I often gave clerks the "wrong" denomination bill, and found that the error was usually greeted honestly and patiently. Most of the time, the cashier pointed out my error and questioned whether I wanted change or meant to provide a different bill.

On at least one occasion, however, I was deliberately and maliciously shortchanged.

I had entered a drugstore to purchase a package of tissues. Not seeing what I wanted, I asked the man behind the counter for assistance. He was young, perhaps nineteen or twenty. Reaching for a display behind him, he placed the package next to the register.

"Will there be anything else?"

"No, thank you, young man," I responded softly, shaking my head and resting my cane against the counter. I placed my handbag on the surface in front of me and opened the clasp slowly. Finding my change purse, I carefully removed three crumpled bills.

After staring at the money for a moment, I handed him a ten-dollar bill.

"Thank you, and your change," he said, counting aloud, as he placed several coins in my still-out-stretched palm. I paused for a moment, shocked by what he had done. I felt it could not have been accidental. I stared at the clerk and waited. Ignoring me, he began to arrange bottles on the shelf behind him.

I placed the coins into my purse, and then, without leaving character, I raised my voice: "And now may I have my nine dollars!"

He stopped his work and turned to me.

"Pardon, ma'am?" he asked innocently.

My voice was firm, with a sharper edge than a woman of eighty-five probably could have managed. "You heard what I said, young man!"

We stood for a moment, our eyes fixed, until he moved toward the cash register. He removed the bills and placed them onto the counter. Nine dollars.

Without saying another word, he turned and resumed shuffling the items on the shelf.

I picked up my money and left.

\*   \*   \*   \*

There were facts of life which I learned quickly as the *Old* Pat Moore. One was a simple economic reality: *old* women with money are treated much differently from *old* women with*out* money. One of my colleagues suggested that I test the effect of socioeconomic level on the treatment my character received, so I developed a wardrobe and persona for three different levels. I appeared on some occasions as a wealthy dowager, with fine clothes and jewelry; on others, I was as an ordinary lower-middle-class woman who was frayed but respectable; and on other occasions, I became one of those poor vagabonds called "bag ladies" who are seen on the streets of many major cities.

The results were predictable: whether one is young or *old,* money talks. If I had the appearance of wealth, I was paid more attention, shown more deference, and given better treatment than I otherwise got.

Although this pattern exists regardless of one's age, it is exaggerated with older people. The dismissal and neglect of the elderly is largely a result of the perception that they have lost power, and are therefore not to be reckoned with, as are the young. The appearance of wealth negates that perceived loss of power; it exempts the older person, to a degree, from being classified as unimportant.

On the other end of the continuum, the poor are usually treated shabbily, whatever their age. But to be poor *and old,* that is a combination which renders an individual virtually invisible to polite society. That is the unfortunate fate of the bag ladies. Treated like vermin whose age and poverty might somehow be contagious, they rarely are the objects of the charitable impulses which other of society's unfortunates receive.

At one point in my life in character, I became intrigued by these outcasts, these elderly women who occupy the lowest rung on America's social caste system. I decided to try to get acquainted with one of them, to find out more. There was one *old* lady whom I had seen almost daily in Central Park in the spring of 1980. She walked through the park, sometimes singing, sometimes talking quietly, not raving or babbling, as others I had seen. She seemed to be a safe choice.

Who are these bag ladies? I wondered. Where do they come from? Why do they live in the streets?

Day after day they walk the streets, some cry or sing, others sit or walk in silence. Day after day they somehow survive. Sleeping on park benches or on the sidewalks, foraging through trash cans, collecting bits and pieces of this and that. Tourists are often startled at the sight of them; city-dwellers learn to ignore them, to look right past them.

Social workers and professionals from government agencies or groups such as the Salvation Army have had difficulty learning much about these women, or providing them with services. They resist most attempts to help or even communicate with them. They seem to fear the overtures of anyone who represents authority or the social establishment.

If these bag ladies would not tell the professionals why they lived as they did, perhaps they would discuss their lives with a peer? I decided it was worth trying.

Having selected a likely candidate for my attempt, I dressed carefully for the day. I put aside my orthopedic shoes in favor of ratsy old slippers. Instead of my usual purse, I carried a tattered paper shopping bag stuffed with clothing, cookies, and fruit. I wore a ragged sweater and a dress that I had purchased for one dollar at a second-hand shop in the East Village.

There was no need for lipstick or rouge that day, and my gloves were soiled and my hose torn. Otherwise, I was in usual character.

I had never seen two bag women together, or witnessed an exchange, so I was uncertain as to how I should initiate contact. I sat on a park bench for over an hour, waiting for her to arrive. She finally did so, ambling over to the bench where I had seen her on previous days.

Taking a deep breath, I leaned over, picked up my bag, and stood. I began to walk slowly toward her.

When I reached her bench I sat down, trying to be as nonchalant as possible, trying not to do anything that might cause her to move away.

We sat, motionless and unspeaking, for about twenty minutes.

I finally made a move. Reaching into my bag, I removed two cookies. I turned my head in her direction; she sat staring, almost lifeless. I stretched my arm toward her, offering one of the cookies. She made no response, showed no recognition of the gesture.

Frozen in my position, I waited until my shoulder ached from the effort.

"Cookie?" I asked simply. "Do you want a cookie?"

Still no movement. No reply.

"They are very good."

Nothing.

So I returned the cookies to my bag and continued to sit quietly. She hadn't moved for half an hour now. In desperation, I decided to sing. Perhaps she would at least show some indication of noticing me if I portrayed the behavior of the more animated women I had seen.

I hummed and chanted and softly sang little ditties, barely above a whisper, until eventually I tired of the effort. Through it all she never looked my way.

Suddenly she moved. She reached for her bags, stood without a word, and walked slowly away.

I felt like following her, grabbing her, doing something from the sheer frustration of being unable to communicate with her in any way. Instead, I sat on the bench and watched until she walked out of sight.

This is a drawing made by Pat Moore years before she decided to go into character. But there is an uncanny resemblance to the character she later developed.

Pat as the "wealthy lady." (Photo by Bruce Byers.)

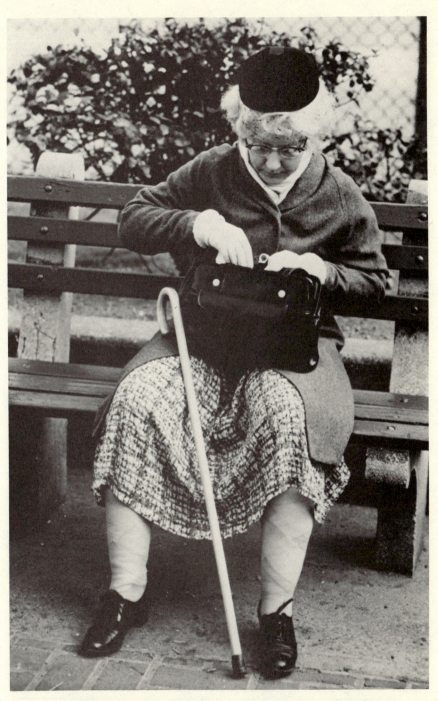

Pat as a "middle income lady." (Photo by Bruce Byers.)

Pat as a "bag lady." (Photo by Bruce Byers.)

## CHAPTER

# 13

NOT ALL MY ATTEMPTS TO COMMUNICATE were so unsuccessful. Some, in fact, were *too* successful, in the sense that they promised to lead to a closer personal friendship than I could sustain while in character.

The more experience I gained, the better I understood the warnings I had received at the PRIM&R conference in Boston.

My severest internal conflicts as the *Old* Pat Moore came when I met those people who were obviously lonely and in need of a friend. I could become only superficially acquainted; it was necessary to terminate the relationship before I got too deeply involved. I felt cruel. Here were people reaching out, trying to connect with another human being who similarly needed friendship, and I was unable to get involved.

I wanted so badly to get to know them better, but I dared not.

On one occasion, I found myself becoming involved in a friendship which, had it continued, might well have become a golden-years romance.

I was sitting in a park, watching pigeons feeding, dogs romping, and children with their mothers, when an *old* man approached and asked if he could join me.

I looked up and squinted into the bright sunlight. Shielding my eyes, I saw the friendly smile of a gentleman about eighty years of age. I nodded my approval, and he sat down.

He had a paper bag in his hand. Opening it, he offered me a piece of hard candy. "They are dietetic, in case you have sugar problems."

"Thank you," I smiled, taking it from him.

I tried to unravel the cellophane wrapper from the candy, but my gloves and stiffened fingers made it difficult. He reached for the brightly colored candy.

"Allow me," he smiled. Carefully unwrapping the candy, he held it between thumb and forefinger and returned it to me.

"My name is Pat."

"Hello, Pat! It's a pleasure to make your acquaintance. I'm George." He tipped his hat.

We sat without speaking, comfortably silent, enjoying the kaleidoscope of activity around us.

"What a beautiful day!" he offered after a few moments, making a show of sniffing the air. "Just smell that air! I do believe fall is coming."

I laughed at his small, comical gesture. "It's been a wonderful summer."

# Chapter 13

"It has," he agreed simply. "I'm looking forward to the fall, though." He looked at me and smiled, as if not to seem argumentative. "I love to watch the leaves turn."

"The colors are so beautiful, especially up North. It's really something to see."

"Oh yes." His enthusiasm swelled, almost visibly, at the thought. "Oh yes indeed. I used to love to take long drives, in the fall of the year, with my wife. We used to go upstate just to see the colors." A short pause. "She's gone now."

As if a drain somewhere deep inside him had been opened, the lightness and easy banter were suddenly gone, leaving a mood I could not quite define, something far sadder and more poignant than mere nostalgia.

I didn't know what to say, so I said nothing.

He continued softly, after a moment's pause, as if deciding I would not object to hearing more. "When she took sick, she said, 'George, life's for the living! You promise me you won't waste it!'" He watched a toddler, on the grass fifty yards away, giggling with her father. He swallowed. "It's hard being alone."

"How long has it been, George?" I asked, choosing my words carefully, still not looking at him.

"Three years and two months."

His voice tightened and wavered, and I felt myself praying, for his sake, that he would not cry.

"The first year, I just sat in the apartment. I didn't want to see anyone, or talk to anyone, or go anywhere. I missed her so much."

He took a handkerchief from the pocket of his jacket. Without looking in his direction, I could see him take a quick swipe at his eyes, as though hoping I wouldn't

109

notice, then return the handkerchief to his pocket. We sat in silence, watching the little girl play, and the moment of tension passed.

"I got myself together, though." He didn't sound very convinced of it.

"I found some groups for people my age. They help a lot. One of them, especially—it's like a singles club, really, although no one calls it that. We take weekend trips and vacations. You're with people you have a lot in common with. That makes it nice."

I smiled in encouragement.

"And then I spend time at the Center. We play cards and talk, and it's very pleasant."

"Do your friends join you?"

His response surprised me. "No," he said forthrightly, with a trace of a nervous smile, "I don't have any friends. Not really."

He was so charming, so outgoing, such a gentleman. Why would he not have friends?

"Well!" he exclaimed, his voice pitched higher and louder, signaling a change in the direction of the conversation. "Enough about me! I've monopolized this conversation long enough. What about you? Are you married, Pat?" As he spoke, he shifted slightly on the bench, turning to face me.

"No," I said, shaking my head. "Not anymore."

"Oh, I'm sorry."

"I think we have something in common, George. I think I know how you feel. It's a strange feeling to love someone, live with someone, and then suddenly be alone. I wonder if I'll ever get accustomed to it."

again, and sat on "our" bench, hoping to see George. It was very important to me to see him again, to know he was all right. I sat there for the rest of the afternoon, watching the usual park happenings—pigeons feeding, dogs romping, and mothers with their children. But I didn't see George.

Perhaps he was ill. Perhaps the doctor had put him in the hospital. Perhaps he was alone and needed my help. Perhaps he had died. I didn't even know his surname.

When the sun started to go down and I made my way from the park, I thought I might start to cry.

I never saw George again. I think I was beginning to understand a small bit of what it was like to be *old*.

"Time heals all," he replied. "Time heals all."

"Is that a promise?"

"That's a promise. Now! Let me get you another lemon drop!"

The mood had been heavy long enough, and we moved onto safer ground. We were strangers, after all, and I think we both were suddenly self-conscious about sharing such private thoughts. We talked and laughed about unimportant things after that, enjoying the companionship, the stories, swapping comments on the human parade that passed through the park before us. Finally the bag of candy, and the afternoon itself, was gone.

We rose to leave.

"I come to the park almost every day in good weather," George said. "Perhaps I'll see you again, Pat?"

"That would be very nice, George. One day next week?"

"Oh, I'd enjoy that!" He seemed delighted.

"I'll come on Tuesday, if the weather is good," I suggested. "This bench?"

"That would be fine!" he agreed. "Why don't we make it twelve o'clock noon, and I'll bring us a nice lunch."

"That would be wonderful. Good-bye, George," I waved back at him as I walked toward the street. "Tuesday!"

"Good-bye, Pat!"

And as I shuffled stiffly down the street, cane in hand, I thought to myself, "Pattie Anne Moore, I believe you just made a date!"

* * * *

It was a date I kept, and so did George. He was waiting on the bench when I arrived a week later, a few minutes before twelve. He was dressed in a rather more dapper fashion than before, it seemed to me, and wore a white carnation in his lapel.

I approached as he was looking in the opposite direction. "George! Hello!" I was glad to see him.

"Pat, oh my goodness!" He spun around and stood, tipping his hat. "I didn't see you coming. You look lovely."

And with that he reached for a bouquet of daisies lying on the bench, presenting them to me with a flourish. I thanked him and we sat down.

George had promised lunch, and lunch he delivered, in a far more elaborate style than I had anticipated. After very little preliminary conversation, he produced a small rattan picnic hamper, and from it he spread on the bench between us a gourmet lunch of chicken salad sandwiches and fruit.

I had omitted the layer of latex which I sometimes wore on my lips, in anticipation of having lunch, but still I had to eat carefully. This was no time for a peeling face. I didn't know how this was going to end—I was beginning to worry about it a little—but I knew I didn't want my face to disintegrate right there with the chicken and the apple slices.

"Tea?" George asked, reaching for a Thermos and a mug. He had thought of everything. It was peppermint tea, decaffeinated.

After lunch, we visited for a couple of hours, then George excused himself. "I've enjoyed it so much, Pat;

I'm sorry we can't visit longer, but I have a doctor's appointment."

"Don't apologize. It's been a lovely lunch."

"May I see you again next week, Pat?" he asked hopefully.

I hesitated. How was I going to handle this? Maybe I shouldn't have gone this far. But he seemed so eager, I hated to refuse, and it had been enjoyable talking with him. Still I was unsure.

"How about next Tuesday?" he pressed ever so gently, eyebrows raised in anticipation of my reply.

*Oh well,* I thought, *one more time won't hurt. And by next week I'll think of a way out of this.* "I'd like that, George," I said finally, smiling to excuse my hesitation. "Same time, same place?"

"Wonderful!" he beamed at me. "I'll see you here next Tuesday at noon. Let me bring lunch again. I'm a very good cook and I like to show off."

"Next week. Good-bye, George."

And with a tip of his hat he was gone, leaving me on the park bench.

* * * *

The next Tuesday I was there again, with a carnation on my lap for George.

I waited until two o'clock for him to arrive. He never came. At first, I wasn't concerned. Perhaps he had been delayed by an errand, or another appointment with his doctor had been necessary. He had no way of making contact with me. But the afternoon passed, and he never arrived.

The next week, Tuesday at noon, I went to the park

# CHAPTER

## 14

I AVOIDED TELLING MY PARENTS ABOUT what I was doing until I was well along in the process. I was not trying to hide it from them so much as trying to keep them from unnecessary worry. They were protective enough of their oldest daughter already, and I didn't want to face their disapproval, even if it were based on simple parental concern.

By the time I finally told them, the experiment was already well established, and they did not attempt to discourage me. But when I offered to let them see me in character, they firmly declined. "I just don't want to see you that way, Pattie Anne," my mother refused emphatically, "I just don't want to see it."

The hard part was telling Dutch. I didn't know how he would react, but I wanted to share it with him. He listened quietly as I explained to him what I was doing, and tears welled up in his eyes. Dutch is not normally one to weep, and it shook me a little. He was eighty-eight years of age at the time. "Be careful, Pattie Anne," he told me. "Oh please be careful." He was afraid for me, and it showed.

I glibly assured him I was being very careful.

I wish I had listened better.

It was not the first time I was warned to be careful, but I never took seriously enough the words of caution. A few months earlier, I was with a group of friends on a social occasion, and found myself talking with a man who was a New York City police officer. In the course of the evening, I told him about my disguise and the way I used it to do research.

His reaction was one of immediate disapproval and concern for my safety. "You could get killed," he stated flatly.

The thought had never entered my mind.

"What do you mean?" I asked.

"Pattie, *old* people are attacked in this town all the time! They get beaten. They get robbed. There are scum out there who enjoy the chance to beat somebody up for a few dollars, or just for the fun of it. You're absolutely crazy to go out alone like that!"

I could see he was serious. His face showed genuine concern, and it gave me pause. I had never thought of myself as a potential victim. And of course I didn't intend to let it discourage me at this point; I was learning too much to stop now.

"Don't do it, Pattie," he repeated several times. "You're setting yourself up for trouble. Please don't go out alone. It just isn't safe."

I appreciated his sincerity, but I shrugged and changed the subject.

Perhaps I ignored these warnings simply because I was naive and innocent. But maybe there was another reason for my resistance: I had begun to venture further and further into parts of town that were considered high-risk areas, and I didn't want to stop. In retrospect, I suspect that I knew I was taking unacceptable chances, and I was just strongheaded enough that I didn't want to listen to people who told me so. I reasoned that I was smart enough to avoid any potentially dangerous situations, so there was nothing to worry about.

Then one day I made a disastrous error in judgment, and I almost paid for it with my life.

I had begun spending time in Harlem. Four or five times previously I had been to that section of New York in character, visiting both the Hispanic and the black areas. I was well aware of Harlem's reputation as a high-crime district, and was careful to go there only in the middle of the day, staying on major streets in well-traveled areas.

To many people, the very word *Harlem* is a synonym for trouble. Some cabbies will not even drive through the area after dark, and for a frail-looking *old* woman to go to that part of town just to walk around may seem patently foolish. But I didn't go to Harlem out of simple stupidity or because I was asking for trouble.

I chose deliberately to spend time in Harlem, in order to share the experience of the many elderly men and women who live there. Some are there by choice, and others are there because they have no alternative. It is a condition which is called "gray ghettoing," these pockets of older residents who are living in neighborhoods which have changed gradually into areas plagued by poverty and crime.

The suburbs are a fairly recent phenomenon in American life. Harlem was once a bustling residential area. Older citizens living there in many cases have grown up, reared their families, sent their husbands off to war, enjoyed many decades in the same houses and apartments. When the neighborhoods deteriorate, becoming populated with largely poor minority residents, many of these older residents are "trapped" by their own limited resources and cannot leave. Others are emotionally unwilling to make the transition. So they stay, living daily with the fear of being victimized by an increasingly hostile subculture.

That is why I wanted to spend time in Harlem as an *old* woman, to get a feel for the experience of people in that circumstance.

But one day I stayed too late. It was early winter, and dark comes quickly in New York City that time of year. I made a mistake and I paid for it.

The day had begun as a typical day for me. I had no need to go to the office or Columbia, so I planned to spend the entire afternoon in character. I allowed myself the luxury of sleeping late that morning, then spent a couple of hours working at the apartment. I did my own makeup and got myself into character, and shortly after noon left to go uptown.

I took my usual route. The nearest subway stop for a train going all the way uptown to Harlem was at the corner of Seventh Avenue and Twenty-third Street. When I was in character, getting to that subway stop—usually a twenty-minute walk—required about an hour.

From my apartment, I walked up First Avenue to where it intersects with Twenty-third Street, then headed west on Twenty-third all the way over to Seventh Avenue. This may be a pleasant, brisk stroll for a young person, but for a woman of eighty-five it can be an ordeal. City streets and traffic lights are not designed or timed for *old* people with canes. Crossing every street presents a challenge. The intersection I dreaded most was where Broadway and Fifth Avenue converge, right at the Flatiron Building. I had to cross that intersection on my way to the subway stop, and there was simply no way for me to get across in the time the traffic light allowed.

Once I got to the subway, I took the hundred-block ride up to 125th Street, where the train comes above ground onto an elevated track, in the middle of Harlem at a major intersection, Broadway and 125th. Leaving the train, I carefully negotiated the long flight of steps down to the street from the elevated train platform.

I spent the afternoon prowling the streets, stores, and small parks of Harlem. It was a cool day, but the sun was shining brightly, and in the middle of the afternoon the temperature rose; it was comfortable to be outdoors. I remember it as a typical Harlem day. The sidewalks were crowded; teenagers walked by with radios blasting; panhandlers begged for money; women walked by with pushcarts full of groceries.

Toward the end of the afternoon, I was getting hungry, and though the crowds on the streets were already beginning to thin, I thought I had time to eat and still get back downtown before dark. I stepped into a little Spanish restaurant, up around 135th Street— I'm not sure exactly.

Inside, I saw that the menu-board, painted up over the grill, was written in Spanish, and I couldn't understand enough of it to order. A teenage boy was there, and he helped me with the menu. I was impressed with his effort to be helpful, and I chatted with him while waiting for the "arroz y pollo" (chicken and rice). The food was good, I was tired, the little restaurant was warm and cozy, and I stayed much too long.

When I stepped outside, I was surprised to see how little daylight was left. It was already dusk, and becoming dark very rapidly now. I headed south, back toward the subway stop, but it was farther than I had realized, and I began to get scared. I decided to leave the main street and head east, intending to get eventually to Park Avenue, where I should be able to hail a cruising cab.

I was walking as fast as I could because for the first time in Harlem I had a sense of danger. In my effort to go across to Park Avenue, I found myself in unfamiliar territory. I had never been here before. Everywhere were dilapidated buildings, graffiti on walls and sidewalks, crumbling concrete steps. The street was empty.

Trying to hurry, I came to a deserted playground, and cut across it diagonally. It was isolated and poorly lit. As I left the street to cut through the playground, I was suddenly filled with fear, almost a premonition. I looked nervously behind me and, wishing I could move faster, walked on across the dirty concrete.

Suddenly I felt a terrific blow, as something slammed into my back, and someone grabbed me roughly around the neck from behind. I was jerked violently backwards, and thrown to the ground. I saw white light, and pain shot through my back and head. I had been a tomboy and a tree climber as a kid, and I had been hurt before, but nothing like this. The pain was so intense I had sensations of almost blacking out, and I struggled not to lose consciousness.

As I went down, involuntarily clutching my purse, one of them yanked it from my grasp, and just as he did I felt a foot slam into my stomach. It knocked the breath from me and I stretched out on the ground in pain, gasping for air.

The boys didn't run when they got the purse. They danced around me, jeering and taunting and kicking me viciously. I didn't think I was going to live through it. I was being beaten, and I had no way to resist; I instinctively curled into a fetal ball. The balsa wood behind my knees had been broken by the initial blow, and I pulled my knees toward my chest and tried to cover my head with my arms.

"Please don't! Please stop!" I whispered, in a voice that was half-crying, half-pleading. But they didn't stop; their feet kept punching, kicking, pounding my body. I don't think I screamed, although I may have. All I remember is lying there as they stomped me, praying for it to stop; and for some reason I remember thinking I was being hurt so badly I would never be able to have a baby.

I remember thinking I was going to die. And then I must have passed out.

When I came to, I was lying on my right side. As consciousness slowly returned, I was aware of lying with my face on the dirty concrete, and I realized that it was over, that I was still alive and they were gone. The attack had been fast and brutal, and as I became aware that it was over, relief swept over me. Then came the pain, like I had never felt before, especially in my back and right side.

I tried to stand and couldn't. My cane was lying

nearby; I got to my hands and knees and crawled over to it, every movement bringing more pain. Using my cane, I struggled upright. I began to walk, shuffling along, sobbing hysterically now as I limped from the playground and down the sidewalk.

I realized I had to get a better grip, had to get hold of myself, and I prayed as I crept along the deserted sidewalk. Gradually, I grew calmer, and my mind cleared. Did I want to go to the police station and report this? *No*, I thought, *what was the point? The purse contained nothing of value; I didn't get a good look at anyone's face; and most of all, how would I explain to the police what I was doing and why I was dressed like an "old" lady? I couldn't face their questions; I just wanted to go home.*

I don't know how long it took. I eventually reached a street where there was traffic, and finally got a taxi to stop. When I got into the back seat of the cab, I blurted out the address of my apartment, then broke down. I didn't stop sobbing until after we arrived.

The taxi driver didn't even ask what my problem was. At the apartment, I reached inside my dress and fumbled with the safety pin which held a small change purse against my chest. I had never used this emergency fund before, but it was still there, intact, and just enough to cover the fare.

Inside my apartment, I crawled up into my bed and cried myself to sleep. I couldn't stop. I was too devastated to deal with it.

The next morning I awoke slowly, and when I tried to move, I hurt everywhere. Every bone and muscle ached. I got to the bathroom, filled my big deep tub with hot water, and somehow got in for a long soak. Only then did I call Barbara.

"Barbara, I'm really hurt." I was crying.

"What's wrong, Pattie?" Barbara asked, practically screaming into the phone.

"I'll tell you all about it, but right now can you come and get me? I'm really hurt, Barbara."

When I saw her, I fell apart emotionally once again. I couldn't stand on my right leg. I knew it was not broken, or I could never have gotten home on it the night before. It had to be nerve damage of some sort, but I couldn't stand on it at all.

Barbara got a taxi, and we went to an orthopedic doctor, who saw me immediately. Barbara took care of everything; I was so traumatized I just was not functioning very well. She filled out all the forms, answered the questions, deflected the doctor's inquiries about how it had happened, and afterwards got me home and into bed.

The orthopedist told me nothing was broken. I was badly bruised all over my torso, legs, and arms, had a pinched nerve in my hip, and had some sciatic nerve damage. The nerves in my left hand were also damaged. Apparently I had taken the major force of the fall on that hand. Today I still wear a splint and brace on my left hand and wrist, and I have two fingers with no feeling.

I gradually got over the physical pain of that mugging, but the attack did something to me from which I still have not fully recovered; it made me fearful. I feel like a coward even to admit it; I am, after all, a veteran New Yorker, a city-dweller for ten years, and I should be able to forget it, but it has stayed with me. I suppose it is every woman's nightmare, and when it happened to me it left an emotional scar.

After that night, I never returned to Harlem; but,

having originally gone there to learn better how *old* people in such areas feel, I must say that my purpose was achieved. I learned something that night about how it feels to be a victim, to be vulnerable and defenseless, to be an easy prey for whoever is out there seeking someone to brutalize.

It is easier now for me to understand why elderly men and women become virtual prisoners in their apartments, afraid to venture out on the streets except when it is absolutely necessary, and then being constantly fearful, never able to relax.

Is this an age-related problem? Of course it is. I had been in Harlem many times as the *Young* Pat Moore. As a researcher for the Brookdale Institute, I had conducted interviews in some of the most depressed parts of Harlem, and had never been uncomfortable or afraid. I was a healthy young woman with a briefcase who looked and felt confident and in control, and I was never threatened in a year of doing that research.

When we were being trained for the Brookdale project, we were given the conventional advice for young women who work in a ghetto area: stand up straight, move briskly and confidently, act like you know what you're doing, and no one will bother you. And that worked. But it is difficult to tell that to a frail woman bent over by osteoporosis—it's hard for her not to look weak and vulnerable. It's hard not to look frightened because you *are* frightened when you're in that situation.

So the *"old"* people stay home, and put three or four locks on each door, and their loneliness and lack of meaning is magnified.

* * * *

It was more than a year later.

I was walking home, in my own neighborhood, and it was nearly dusk. I was in character, and I was tired, and all I could think was that in another few blocks I would be home.

As I walked past a church, I realized that I wasn't alone. I recognized the muffled sound of footsteps behind me.

I tried to quicken my pace.

"Lady," a voice called from behind me.

I jerked to a halt, afraid. My breathing all but stopped. I stood motionless, realizing that whoever had called to me was running now. And the sound of running feet told me he was not alone—there was more than one of them.

Terrified, I tried to run, but I was an *old* lady of eighty-five, and I couldn't move. I heard myself give a little moan, and tried to go faster.

I felt him touch me on the arm. I stiffened.

"Lady," he repeated, coming around to face me now.

He stared at me, obviously puzzled by my look of horror and fear. "You dropped this," he said, smiling to reassure me and reaching for my hand. He gently pushed a lace handkerchief into my clenched fist.

I closed my eyes in relief.

"Are you all right, lady?" he asked with concern.

"Yes, thank you. Thank you very much." My voice was quivering, and I felt like I might cry.

"Okay." He smiled, turned to his friends, and off they ran.

It had been over a year since that night in Harlem,

but still the brutal experience was so fresh it haunted me. Not every day. Not when I was the Young Pat Moore. But on those days when I was *old* and bent and slow, the fear came back, the sense of helplessness and vulnerability.

I had truly come to understand the tears, the terror that I saw in the eyes of *old* people who shared their stories of burglaries and muggings—real or merely anticipated.

It was a hard-won empathy. I had set out to gain a better understanding, and I was getting it; but, like most things of value, it was not coming easily.

# CHAPTER
# 15

THROUGHOUT 1980 AND '81, I CONTINUED MY work with the empathic character. Being in the role of the *old* woman kept me on a roller coaster of contrasting emotions. There were countless times of frustration and anger—frustration at the physical constraints and weaknesses of the aging body, and anger at the generally insensitive way so many young people ignore and underestimate the older people around them.

But for every negative experience, there was an equally positive one; for every episode which showed me the downside of being *old,* there was an experience in which I could feel the depth of mutual caring, the interpersonal richness, which characterizes life for so many older people.

There were times when I didn't live up to the image

of the spunky Pat Moore—times when I just couldn't find the emotional resources to assume the character of the *Old* Pat Moore, times when I never made it out the door. Once in Chicago, I went through the entire process of going into character, left my hotel room as I had done so many times, went out on the street, and simply panicked. I stood on the sidewalk for a minute or so in front of the hotel, embarrassed to admit to myself that I was afraid, and then finally went back up to my room and stayed. Why was I frightened? I was afraid of getting hurt. It was that simple.

Fortunately, such times were rare. In city after city, I walked the streets, rode the buses and taxis, sat in the parks, and visited the neighborhoods. Sometimes I would check into a hotel or motel as the *Old* Pat Moore and check out as the *Young* Pat Moore, or vice versa. When it was a small motel, with the same desk clerks, it caused a certain amount of confusion. I never offered an explanation, and never had to give one.

Occasionally I would encounter attractive young men—without wedding rings!—who would go out of their way to treat the *Old* Pat Moore with tender, patient concern. I was single and very eager for male companionship at the time, and it seemed such a waste to have all this attention, from a marvelous-looking and apparently eligible young man, lavished on me when I was not in a position to enjoy it!

At times like that, I would fantasize tearing off my wig and ripping away the latex wrinkles and introducing him to the real me!

I shared this dilemma with one of the *old* women who lived in my neighborhood, a good friend who knew about the character. She suggested a unique solution. What I should do, she said, was carry a picture of my younger self in my purse when I was in the *Old* Pat Moore role. When I met a nice eligible bachelor, I was to remove the photo from my bag, show him what a "lovely granddaughter" I had, and explain that I knew he would adore meeting her.

I never had the nerve.

## CHAPTER

# 16

THE FIRST TIME I HEARD ABOUT PHYSICAL abuse of the elderly was while I was in college. One of the girls from the dorm earned money during the summer months by working in a nursing home.

In one of those rambling gab sessions in the dorm late one night, she talked about the elderly people with whom she worked: "They're so drugged and senile that you have to slap them around so they'll listen," she laughed. "And if they wet the bed more than once during my shift, I just let them sleep in it. I'm not cleaning that mess again." She was almost boastful.

"Oh, no!" I exclaimed in horror. "How can you possibly do that?"

"If you worked with them, you'd see," she insisted defensively. "You wouldn't be able to stand them either."

I was stunned by what I was hearing.

"Those are people," I pleaded. "You can't just treat them any way you want!"

"It doesn't matter, Pattie," she said, with a tone that let me know the conversation was over. "They don't know the difference anyhow."

That was the first hint I had of a problem which most experts insist is a rapidly growing national health hazard: the physical abuse of the elderly. Between 1979 and 1982, talking with older men and women around the country, I heard many stories of such abuse, occurring not just in nursing homes, but at the hands of spouses and, most often, the victim's own children.

When I mention this problem in a public forum, people recoil almost visibly. It is one of those conditions which is the object of massive public denial; it is so horrible that civilized people just don't want to think about it. We want to pretend it is not there, and hope that it will magically go away.

Abuse of the elderly has reached such proportions that it has been the subject of a six-year study by a subcommittee of the Select Committee on Aging of the United States House of Representatives.

Representative Claude D. Pepper, the congressman from Florida who has been linked to many legislative initiatives to help the elderly (he is himself eighty-four), says: "No one has really recognized how widespread this terrible problem is. The truth is that no one *wanted* to recognize it. We ignored it because it was just too horrible to accept. We didn't want to believe that things like this could take place in a civilized nation."

In an investigative report published in *Parade* magazine in early 1985, journalist Donald Robinson estimated that one of every twenty-five *old* people is abused. The average age of the victim is seventy-five or older, he said, and the victim is more likely to be a woman than a man. He quotes Dr. Suzanne K. Steinmetz, a professor at the University of Delaware and an authority on abuse of the elderly: "The situation is getting worse because people are living longer and are not economically productive anymore. Their families have to care for them and don't know how. Many lose control out of frustration."

I talked once with a woman whom I considered to be the personification of the perfect grandmother— white hair beautifully styled, twinkling blue eyes, and an infectious smile. We had met through a mutual friend, who told me she wanted to hear more about my work. While other people were around, her interest in my work was entirely professional and impersonal. She was impressed with what I was doing, she said, and she simply wanted to know more about it.

When we finally had the opportunity to talk privately, however, after almost a full day together, she admitted to me that she had a more personal reason for wanting to see me. She was in great personal pain, she said, and she wanted to talk about it.

I told her I was glad to listen.

She had trouble saying it. She turned her head and looked out the window. Finally she spoke.

"My husband hurts me . . . he hurts me," she said in a quiet, embarrassed voice, still looking away.

I waited for her to continue.

"I hate him. I wish he would just die so I could have some happiness in my last years. I wish he would just go away!"

She looked up and her eyes were filled with tears.

I took her hand, and after she composed herself a bit, she told me of the malignant spiral of his abuse, which triggered her own hatred of him, which left her with enormous guilt. She believed only her husband's death would gain her release from a life of abuse; she saw no other way out. And to have such feelings, to wish for his death, filled her with such self-loathing that it seemed to her sometimes that she, not he, was the bad person in their house.

She was afraid of him. They slept in separate rooms, and barely spoke, but he would drink, and then the abuse would begin.

Did their children know?

"No! Oh no!" She exclaimed. "They worship their father, and I could never ruin that. It didn't begin happening until long after they left home, so they have never known about it. But I could never bring them into this. Never!"

I suggested the obvious—that she move out. But she was trapped, she said. Divorce was out of the question; her religion did not allow it, and she was "too *old*" in any event. And for anyone to know would mean too much disgrace, for her as well as her husband. She'd rather die than have people know.

She had no place to go. She had no way to support herself. She had resigned herself to her terrible life because she was too *old,* she thought, to have any options but to stay and try to cope as best she could.

She had seen in me the opportunity to tell someone that she was in pain, and to ask if hers was an isolated case, if perhaps she was not alone. A chance to talk it out, that's all she wanted, she said, and nothing more.

And in fact, as she left me, though I was frustrated at my inability to help, she did appear more at peace.

The tragedy is that she saw her age as her jailer—an incommutable sentence to a life of unhappiness.

The trap in which abused older people find themselves is tightened by their financial and emotional dependence on the very persons who abuse them. Their social isolation cuts them off from the normal support systems—friends, neighbors, or social agencies—which are available for abused children or battered spouses. And they usually feel that, since they are old and unimportant, no one really cares.

I was sitting in Stuyvesant Park, at Second Avenue and Sixteenth Street, one day. I was in character. There was an older woman sitting on a park bench near me who was visibly upset. She was crying, and my heart went out to her. I walked over to her, sat down on the bench, put my hand on hers, and asked if she needed help. It was as if my question opened the floodgates; the tears that were a trickle became a stream, and she sat and sobbed, no longer attempting to hold them back.

"Why does she do it?" she sobbed, over and over. "Who?" I asked quietly, as she became calmer. "Why does *who* do it?"

"My daughter—why does she beat me?" she cried.

I felt her sadness, her sense of forlorn, unloved dependence. I just sat and held her in my arms for a while, as she told me her story of abuse. Could I help? No. Could I call the police, or get someone else involved? Oh, no, please don't do anything like that.

That day I understood that the physical pain of being beaten was only half as hurtful as the pain in her heart, that it was her own daughter who victimized her so. The abuse, plus the loneliness and humiliation at being so unloved—it is a tragedy doubled and magnified.

What bothered me most about the abused elderly people I met is this: Their perception that no one cares very much about their plight is basically accurate. I had come to feel that the most neglected segment of our population is the elderly, and that most younger people, including the ones with whom I worked and socialized, were too busily preoccupied with their own careers and plans to want to know about the millions of elderly people or the conditions in which they live.

I began to take it personally.

I was coming to identify so fully with the *Old* Pat Moore that I felt more like her than like the real me, and as I did, I began to resent the young, healthy, carefree members of my own generation. Psychologically, as far as my own internal well-being was concerned, it was not a good situation.

I would walk down the street and see the faces of young people like myself, and frustration and anger would well up inside me. I felt like grabbing them and shaking them and saying, "You have no idea what's going on out there, in this very city, with so many precious *old* people who just want you to take a little time with them!"

That anger was wrong, of course. It was wrong to get so overinvolved emotionally, and it was wrong to harbor the anger I felt. It was self-righteous and counter-productive. But it was the sincere anger of one whose eyes had been opened to a world far different from that of tennis games and ski weekends and wine-and-cheese parties at the Country Club. I had been to that different world, and it had changed me. I had begun this project as an industrial designer, and found myself in danger of becoming an overheated crusader.

For Pat Moore, young version or *old*, there was too much pressure building in the internal system. I was nearing a point of emotional and physical burnout. Some of my friends could see the warning signals. I was pushing too hard, working too many hours, trying to carry too much of the burden.

God had brought me down this road for a purpose, and He wasn't going to let me self-destruct. After eighteen months in character, eighteen months of constantly increasing stress, something happened to slow me down.

CHAPTER

# 17

IN DECEMBER OF 1980, A WEEK OR SO BEFORE
Christmas, I had an experience which showed me that
the strain of living in two worlds could not continue.

It happened right at the end of the fall semester
at Columbia University—the semester when I had carried the heaviest academic load of my graduate program. Final exams had begun, and I was into one of
those workaholic binges that had always got me
through.

I was doing the job at the Ellies design firm, going
to classes at Columbia, and had become so obsessive
about my empathic role that I was going into character
at every possible opportunity.

And on top of the scheduling overload, there was
the emotional factor. The whole experience of the empathic character had become more stressful after the

Harlem mugging; my growing sense of identification with the *old* people I represented had given it all an intensity that was exhausting.

I went into final exams that week with some catching up to do. I knew I would have to pull a couple of all-nighters to make it. But I was accustomed to working through the night, as most graduate students are. I would sit up and study all night, drinking coffee and eating M&M's. (It sounds weird, but someone had told me that the caffeine from chocolate gets into your system faster than from drinking coffee. I don't know if it is true or not, but I believed it, so my routine when I studied all night was to double up on caffeine by eating M&M's *and* drinking coffee.)

I was sitting up in bed in the middle of the night, studying for a final exam the next day. I fell asleep sitting upright in bed, book in my lap, and a few minutes later I awoke with such a strong feeling of emotional pressure that I became physically ill. I realized I had reached a state of total exhaustion that was becoming dangerous. I felt unable to deal with matters at hand, unable to make decisions. I felt a rising tide of panic.

I reached for the phone and called Helen, a friend who lived a couple of blocks away. She mumbled a sleepy "hello," and without telling her anything more, I asked her to please come quick. She was there in less than five minutes.

When Helen arrived and saw what shape I was in, she called another friend, and the two of them took me to a Manhattan hospital. The last thing I remember was being wheeled into the emergency room, although Helen tells me that I kept protesting to her and the orderlies that I had an exam the next day and they must not let me miss it.

When I awoke, it was the next afternoon. The exam was at 2:00 P.M., and I had already missed it. I awoke with a doctor standing over my bed—just like in the movies—who introduced himself and told me that I was in a state of "complete exhaustion." He wanted to keep me in the hospital for a few days of observation and tests, and I had little choice but to agree with him.

It all made for a rather dreary Christmas season that year.

Incidentally, I never did take that exam, nor any others that semester. I was in the hospital during the entire exam week, so the university waived my exams and allowed my professors to give me a grade based on work during the semester. With every cloud, as they say, comes a silver lining.

And when I analyze the situation honestly, there was an even more important silver lining for me in the ordeal, and that was the immediate and permanent impact which the near-breakdown had on my approach to my work. I had plenty of time in that hospital room to reflect on what I was doing, and what *it* was doing to me.

When I took a hard look at the pace I was working, and the emotionally frayed condition I had reached, I did not like what I saw. I had always been stoic, not given to tears except in rare situations. But I had become a crier. When I saw lonely people, walking along the street, sitting and watching the rest of the world go by, I felt so much more deeply for them, and it moved me literally to tears.

I had always been a caring person, but not one who falls apart in the presence of pain or grief. Now I would return to my apartment from being with lonely *old* people, or from a visit to a nursing home, and I would break up emotionally. Sometimes I would come in and sit down in my apartment at dusk, and just sit there, without even changing out of character, virtually catatonic, until it got dark. I felt the depth of their need so profoundly, and was so frustrated at my inability to help them.

That changed after December of 1980. My crisis at Christmastime slowed me down; it made me think. I came out of the hospital and headed into 1981 with a better sense of proportion about what I could and could not accomplish. It was one of those mental watersheds in one's life, when I made peace with my own limitations, admitted that I could not save the world single-handedly, and moved on.

I didn't reduce my time spent in character. For another year and a half I continued to take every opportunity to spend time as the *Old* Pat Moore, but I definitely learned to relax more, enjoy it more, and keep the Young Pat Moore in a little better shape.

\* \* \* \*

I was in Florida later that winter, and at the end of an afternoon in character, I decided to take a walk along the beach. As was often the case, I had been saddened by some of the things I had seen and heard that day, and I wanted time alone to process it, to sort out my thoughts, before returning to my hotel room.

I noticed a larger than usual flock of seagulls hovering nearby, attracted by a little boy who was busily throwing pieces of bread into the air. He had torn several slices of bread into small pieces, and was throwing them to the gulls, a delighted grin on his face. He was so involved in the effort that he didn't see me approach, and was startled by my "hello."

"Hi!" he responded cheerfully. "I'm feeding the birds."

I stayed to watch, until the last piece of bread was gone. He gestured to the birds, who still hovered: "They'll stay here until they're sure I don't have no more food."

The teacher in me arose. I couldn't help myself. "*Any* more," I corrected him. "It's 'until I don't have *any* more food.' "

"All right," he said, and his grin reappeared. It was obvious he had heard that correction before.

"Do you live around here?" I asked.

"No, I'm visiting my grandparents. They live over there," he answered, pointing to a row of houses lining the beach.

It was cool that day, much too cool for swimming, and I commented on it to the boy, eager to find a way to keep the conversation going. "It's a shame you can't go swimming today."

"Oh, that's okay," he chirped. "Anyway, I like to look for shells. I've been collecting shells a real long time. I've got lots and lots of them!"

"When did you start?"

"Ever since I was four!"

"How old are you now?"

"Six!" He said it proudly.

He apparently had sized me up and decided we could be friends, and his next question surprised me. "Do you want a cookie?" he asked suddenly.

I declined with a shake of my head, saying, "No, thank you."

"Do you have diabetes too? My grandma has diabetes, and she can't eat cookies neither."

He was so sweet I didn't even correct his grammar. "No," I told him. "I'm just too fat to eat cookies."

"I don't think you're fat," he said sincerely.

I was in love.

"Do you want to look for shells with me?" he asked, looking up hopefully in my direction.

"That would be nice, thank you."

He squatted, picking up his crumpled paper bag from the sand. It held his selection of cookies and a package of bubble gum. We began to walk along the shore.

"Now, if you want to find the good ones," he instructed me, "you have to look real good. If I see the edge of one buried in the sand, I kick at it and get it loose. You can use your cane."

One of his grandparents uses a cane, I thought.

"Like this?" I asked, gouging at a half-buried shell with the end of my cane.

"Yeah, that's good," he answered approvingly. "Now when you see one you want, tell me and I'll pick it up and put it into this bag."

And so we strolled down the beach, poking at the sand in our respective manners, as he talked about his school, his mother and father, and his home in Michigan. He talked about his friends; he told me about the boys on his baseball team. We were buddies.

I realized we had been walking for almost an hour,

and reluctantly told him I thought we should turn around and walk back toward his home.

"Yeah," he agreed, "it's getting time for dinner! Do you want to come with me?"

"No, thank you, sweetheart. I've really enjoyed our walk and talking with you, but I must go back to the hotel now."

"Okay."

I assumed that I wasn't the first friend he had made on the beach and knew I wouldn't be the last. He was absolutely charming!

We reached the place on the beach where we had met. "See?" he threw out his hands. "The gulls are all gone!"

I nodded. "Maybe they're having dinner with someone else!"

We laughed, and he reached for my hand, wrapping his sandy little fingers around mine. I was touched by the spontaneity of his affection.

He knelt on the beach, pouring the contents of the bag near my feet.

"What are you doing?" I asked.

"I have to give you your shells," he said, as if surprised at my question.

"Oh, please, you don't have to do that. I'd like you to keep them for your collection."

He grinned up at me. "Okay, thanks!" He picked a tiny shell from the pile and put the rest back into the bag. "Here, you take this one. It was your favorite."

"Are you sure you don't want it?"

"No, it's okay. You keep it. I've got lots of those."

"Thank you," I said, and bent over to accept the shell. As I did, he reached up and kissed my cheek.

"Bye!" he shouted, as he turned and ran across the

sand. He stopped at the edge of the beach, turned again, and waved good-bye.

For my six-year-old friend, there were no young or *old*, no victims or stereotypes, no barriers of age at all. There was just friendship, and laughter, and a big wonderful beach with plenty of shells for two friends to share.

For me, at the end of a long and tiring day, it was honey for the heart.

# CHAPTER

## 18

I OFTEN THINK BACK TO THAT BOY ON THE beach, especially when I am tempted to become pessimistic or discouraged. I recall the simple, accepting attitude of the boy of six, and of many other youngsters I met while in character, and take heart.

So many problems of older Americans could be solved if the attitudes and perceptions of younger Americans were changed. Not all the problems of aging will disappear with change of attitude, to be sure. A person's physical abilities will still diminish with age, for example, as will the role he or she plays in the work force. But many of the aging individual's emotional and relational problems are produced primarily by the attitudes of others toward them.

The core attitude—that older people are useless, that their lives are over—is reinforced by the youth-obsessed media and advertising community. The message is clear: Young is good; *old* is bad. In my travels in character, I met hundreds of healthy, capable elderly people who expressed the belief that the future was for the young—that their time had passed.

Of course, the majority of older Americans are able to live active lives, bolstered by their talents and skills, their friendships and outlets. My concern is not so much for them. My fears are for the homebound, self-imposed prisoners afraid or unable to leave the relative protection of their dwellings. My concern is for those who are alone and in desperate need of companionship and caring. It is for those who feel that their lives are over because their bodies are bent, their eyesight is failing, their families are grown and gone, their spouses are dead.

Those are the Americans to whom we need to reach out—those who have lost faith and confidence because they are called *"old."*

The novelist Trevanian recently wrote that "the most brutalizing effect of prejudice is that the victims come to believe, at a deep and unconfessed level, the stereotypes established by the oppressor."

That principle may be truer in respect to elderly people than in any other form of prejudice, since the older person, before joining that "minority group," spends sixty-five or seventy years being conditioned to accept the stereotypical view.

A black individual never knows the feeling of being *non*-black; short people don't get that way after first being tall; but elderly people find themselves a part of that category after a lifetime of being "non-elderly." As younger people, they have readily accepted, or even participated in, the negative attitudes toward the eld-erly—they have, after all, no reason to resist them. So when they become the *object* of these stereotypes, they often submit readily to them.

The popular portrayal of older people in the media is part of this problem, and that is why I do not regard such blatantly offensive examples as the Wendy's Clara Peller commercial to be harmless and funny. The Clara Peller character barges into the hamburger joint as the classic stereotype of an *old* woman who is deaf, abusive, and rude. It is a horribly insensitive portrayal. Can you imagine a racial or ethnic stereotype being used in that way to sell hamburgers? The black commu-nity would raise such a strong objection—and rightly so—that it would be taken off the air immediately.

But somehow, aging stereotypes are still socially ac-ceptable, and they are an important factor in the main-tenance of the very attitudes which make life for the elderly so difficult in our society.

That is why I spoke out against the Wendy's commer-cials while they were airing, and urged people to write letters to the company and to the networks in protest. I have had some older people tell me they were not offended by the commercials, that they thought the Clara Peller character was "cute," but the senior citi-zens who expressed that view were all healthy and young-looking individuals. The kids I talked to about it understood, when I asked them, "Is that what your grandmother is like?"

The Wendy's commercial is not the only example, of course. I single it out for mention because it is one of those cases in which the disability of older people is used for comic effect. Its producers want us to sit around our television sets and laugh at the pre-senile *old* woman. When one stops to think about it, that is a sad way to sell hamburgers.

Generally, too many movies and television shows fail to show older people as positive, functioning parts of society, and instead build off older characters by showing them as deficient in some way—deaf, easily confused, crochety, or totally passive. This kind of stereotyping is as bad as the old Hollywood pattern of showing all blacks as maids, butlers, and tapdancers.

There have been initiatives taken recently by such groups as the Gray Panthers and the American Association of Retired Persons to call attention to this problem, and the entertainment industry is responding. Unfortunately, the approach taken most frequently has been to seek out the most stunning examples of senior citizens and use them in commercials which pitch products to older people. Cary Grant and Joan Collins are two good examples.

This approach is certainly better than the Clara Peller type of casting, but it still misses the point. It does not show *old* people as deficient, but on the other hand it sets up another set of unattainable role models for the average man and woman of seventy. George Burns, for example, is a healthy, active older American. But to show him in a television commercial, with a gorgeous young model in a bikini on each arm, does nothing to help the public perception of older people. It merely sets Burns up as a dramatic exception to the existing stereotype, and says, in effect, "If you can be *old* without looking or acting *old*, like George Burns, you can still attract young nubile girls at the poolside."

What good does that do a less famous individual?

What we need in the media are more examples of typical older citizens who are active and making valuable contributions to intergenerational situations. We have a few of those, but not enough. (One television series which showed older people in that context was "The Waltons.") We also will be seeing, I predict, commercials and magazine ads for mainstream products—not just denture cream and senior-citizen passes—which feature older models.

There is a lot of deeply ingrained, unconscious resistance to be overcome, but I am optimistic about the progress that is being made. Ads are generally aimed at the twenty-five to forty-five age group, and *old* has come to be a negative word. I picked up a magazine recently and saw an ad for hair color which promised the reader, in bold letters, that using this product means, "YOU'LL NEVER BE OLD!" *Old* has become a synonym for being useless, ugly, unimportant, of less value. That is the core perception which must be changed, and I think will be changed, in this generation.

## CHAPTER

# 19

AN OBVIOUS WAY TO COMBAT THE NEGATIVE attitudes toward older people is to prevent them from developing in the first place, to teach children about aging in such a way that they never lose the natural acceptance which was displayed by my little friend on the beach in Florida.

Why can young children usually be counted on to offer such acceptance? Because they have not yet learned that elderly people are "different" in any critical way. Unless children have already been tainted by adult attitudes, they have an innocence which makes them good companions for older people.

When kids show fear or lack of acceptance of *old* people, it is usually because they have already been exposed to some of the negative models in our culture. Television is not the only culprit; consider the variety of *old* crones and witches which populate the storybooks in the typical nursery: the witch in *Hansel and Gretel* who lures little children into her house to eat them; the *old* woman in *Snow White* who tries to kill her younger, prettier rival; even the sweet little ol' Grandma turns out to be a wolf in *Little Red Riding Hood.* Have you ever considered how many small children have been traumatized by the Wicked Witch of the West in *The Wizard of Oz?*

The point is not that these stories should not be used, or that a wonderful film like *The Wizard of Oz* should not be shown to youngsters, but that in our culture it is commonplace for *old* people to be portrayed as strange, sinister characters who live alone and don't like little kids very much.

I am often asked by parents who are concerned about the issues of aging in our society, "What can I do as a parent to help my child develop positive feelings and attitudes toward *old* people?" Actually, in addressing the needs of our children, we improve our own self-concept and our ability to relate to others.

I must preface whatever suggestions I make by acknowledging that I have never been a parent. But I hope, God willing, to be one someday; and when I am, here are some of the guidelines I will try to follow:

(1) *When a child notices that the elderly look and act somewhat differently from younger people, and begins to quiz you about the difference, take time to talk about it.* This will often occur when your child physically encounters an older person, whether that person is a stranger in a public place such as a grocery store, church, or the like, or a relative with whom he or she is not well acquainted.

If your child asks questions about why that person

walks with a cane or is in a wheelchair or dresses in an unusual fashion or merely looks different, don't gloss over the truth about aging. Take the time to explain that there are many physical changes which are age-related (such as arthritis, osteoporosis, failing eyesight, the probability of strokes, etc.), that they are normal, and that people who show evidence of them are not to be pitied or feared.

Another common parental tendency is to whisk children from the physical presence of *old* people if the child begins to ask questions about them. But what's better in situations like this is for the parent to relax; the older person will rarely object to a child's well-meaning questions. It's also important not to react too strongly if the child seems uncomfortable with old people. Relax with it; it is probably a simple fear of the unfamiliar. In contemporary times, many young children have literally never been in the presence of older people. And if you yourself are one of those people who are uptight around older people, relax with your own discomfort. To some degree, all of us have had such fears and uneasiness, but by enhancing our own awareness, we become more sensitive and caring individuals.

(2) *Provide your children with as much contact as possible with older people, in as many different positive situations as possible.*

Unfortunately, the housing patterns which are most common today have a tendency to reduce the exposure children have to elderly people. This is one of the worst features of suburban life; it creates neighborhoods in which all the homeowners are of similar age and background. If a child is sixteen years of age before he or she sees an elderly person up close, the likelihood is much greater that the child will see them in an unsympathetic way.

When I was a child, I saw the older people in our neighborhood as part of the normal social landscape. I saw them as potential playmates, not as old people. One of the positive things about traditional neighborhoods is the normal availability of older Americans in the environment.

The desire of middle-aged, middle-class couples to live in homogeneous suburban neighborhoods is not the only factor which contributes to housing patterns in which *old* people are an oddity. On the other side of the continuum, the popularity of retirement communities—the "Sun City phenomenon," it has been called—is also a factor.

There is a trend toward retirement communities in which the rules against children are so strict that grandchildren can visit only with prior permission. This kind of housing arrangement attracts older people with plenty of money who don't want little tykes running around making noise and messing up their lawns. The result is the same as that of the suburbs: hermetically sealed environments in which the whole life span is not represented, and that is not a healthy arrangement.

The caste system in this country is alive and well. Too many of us are too eager to limit our social circle to people of our own kind, and we all miss a lot of life's richness that way. In regular contact with a wide variety of age groups, we enjoy lives which are fuller and more interesting. In modern society, this diversity often means going out of one's way to create the opportunity, but it can be worth the effort—for you as well as your kids.

(3) *Let your child see you reaching out to older people of your acquaintance.* Perhaps the most reliable prediction in child rearing is that your children will learn best the behaviors which you model for them. Personal example is still the best teacher.

Some of my best memories of my father, when I was growing up, are of those times when he would take his tool box and go down the block to the widow Mrs. Becker's house to repair her clothes dryer. If not her dryer, it might be someone else's light socket, or doorknob. He let me tag along, and after the repairs were done, we would usually wind up eating a piece of pie, because Mrs. Becker—or whoever we visited—knew we were coming and had it ready.

That is the way Dad often spent his day off, and he seemed to enjoy it, not only playing Mr. Fix-It for all the older people on the block, but also the conversation afterward. It was only after I became older that I realized that the doorknob was not nearly as important to what Dad was doing as the friendship and the time he shared with these people. They were his friends, regardless of their age; they mattered to him, and it showed.

Every parent can teach that same lesson. Look around your neighborhood. There is probably a widow down the block whom you see sitting on her porch, or an older man who walks his dog past your house. Do you take the time, when your child is with you, to stop and talk with them?—not just say "hello," or nod politely, but do you really take the time to communicate?

154

Find out about that older person with whom you are casually acquainted. Does she need a ride to the grocery store every week? Would she like to babysit? Give her a call next time you are going to the shopping mall for a couple of hours, and see if she might like to go or if perhaps there is something you can bring her. These things seem so simple, but most often they are not done because they require planning and a bit of inconvenience.

A child whose parent models an active interest in older people will learn that older people are valuable, and learn it as naturally as learning to walk.

(4) *Use older citizens to help your child have a sense of "living history."*

One of the greatest gifts older people can give us is their personal recollection of the past. Nothing gives children a sense of the continuity of history with the present like knowing and hearing personally from people who can span the gap with their own memories. Living history is a wonderful form of intergenerational bonding, and families, as well as schools and communities, should make use of it.

This can be done in a fashion as simple as providing opportunities for your children to hear from their grandparents—or other *old* people whom they know— about specific events and conditions in the past. Elderly people usually assume that no one, especially young children, wants to hear their stories. The children themselves do not know to ask. This is one of those activities which must be initiated and structured by the parent, who brings together *old* and young in a relaxed setting with a particular agenda, at least for the first time or so.

When I was a child, we grandkids always looked forward to the time after dinner at Dutch's house because that's when we would gather around to hear him tell stories of the "good ol' days." My mother would get us together and get things started: "Dad, tell the kids about the first time you saw Babe Ruth. . . ."

Dutch never disappointed us. He sat there in his chair for a moment, pulled his baseball cap off his head, stroked his forehead as he pondered, then he would begin: "Well, kiddos . . ." And he would tell the story.

It was no big deal, the story itself, but he was a Yankee fan, and he had seen Ruth once, and it made history live for us. It also made Dutch a more vital person, a person more connected to us, a person of greater value and more depth. And in Dutch's case, it was also invariably entertaining.

Today, a parent can use cassette tapes, video recorders, scrapbooks, all sorts of devices to extend the role of older people as sources of living history to their children. In 1985, an individual who is seventy years of age was already twenty-five when World War II was beginning, and that is ancient history to children. One need not have seen Roosevelt or Hitler to talk about those times of rationing, fireside chats, and all the boys going off to war.

It is difficult for children to imagine an *old* man or woman as ever having been an active, important part of the world. Particularly if elderly people are physically limited or just not around very much, they can seem unidimensional and disconnected—little more than a part of the furniture—to young children who identify people according to the ongoing roles they play.

Involving the older person as the storehouse of living history is an excellent way to change that condition. It is a double-win situation; it gives the older person a way of being valuable and needed, and it also makes an irreplaceable contribution to the child's sense of history and personal continuity.

# CHAPTER

## 20

PRODUCING A GENERATION OF YOUNGSTERS who value and appreciate older people is the long-term solution to the problems of an aging population. In the meantime, however, there is plenty that can be done immediately to improve the quality of life for older Americans.

I am first and foremost an industrial designer. That is where my interest in gerontology began, and it is still the primary focus of my efforts on behalf of older citizens. Speaking strictly in terms of the free market system, the above-sixty-five generation has more going for it today than ever before. The reason: an unprecedented demographic bulge in the United States, in which senior citizens comprise the fastest-growing segment of our society.

There are many ways to plot this trend statistically.

Perhaps the most impressive is this: The *percentage* of Americans over the age of sixty-five will double by the year 2030. Today approximately one American in ten is in that category, but by the year 2030, one of every five Americans will be so classified.

And if the year 2030 is too far away to get one's attention, consider this: The number of Americans over the age of eighty-five will double by the year 2000! By that same year, half of everyone now over fifty will be over seventy-five years of age.

The trend toward an older population has been called the "graying of America," and its impact will be far greater than can be grasped merely by citing statistics. The real story is not so much in the growth of the over-sixty-five population, as in the dramatic rise in the number of citizens much *older* than that.

In America, power seems to follow money and votes, and senior citizens will have an increasing percentage of both as we move into the 1990s and on toward the twenty-first century. By the year 2025, those over sixty-five, who traditionally register and vote at a higher rate than any other identifiable demographic group, will represent fully one-third of the voting population. And already, people over fifty control nearly half of discretionary income in the United States.

Such a welter of numbers is difficult for the average person to digest, but the bottom line is that senior citizens cannot be regarded any longer as a small minority of Americans to be easily ignored. Individuals who are uncomfortable around older people, or who have difficulty relating positively to them, will find themselves more and more out of step in a society whose definition of *old* must inevitably change.

One segment of America which has been surprisingly slow to get that message is the business and corporate community. Despite our national tradition of private philanthropy and voluntarism, the business sector rarely makes policy on the basis of love and good will. From the time of my first attempts to design products with older consumers especially in mind, I have understood that industry will only give full attention to the needs of the elderly when the forces of the marketplace demand it.

Joel Garreau, a Canadian social critic, somewhat cynically describes it this way: "Greed is a far more reliable and universal agent of change than is the urge to do good for your fellow man. The future of any great idea is always made more bright when it's found to be profitable."

The young-is-beautiful mindset of corporate America has been difficult to change, but the companies and merchants who catch the vision of designing specifically for older people will reap rich rewards for their efforts.

Up until now, older Americans have been forced to cope with what I call "Darwinian design"—products designed for the fittest and healthiest consumers. Everything from the design of the product itself, to the packaging of that product, to the way it is shelved in the retail store, assumes that the person who uses it will be strong and healthy.

Older people struggle to reach the box of arthritis medicine off the top shelf at the drugstore; then they struggle to read the label which is printed in small letters in colors difficult for their aging eyes; then they struggle to get the cap off the bottle when they get it home. And this is a product used primarily by older people!

There are so many ways in which we can improve the quality of life for older Americans by designing with their needs in mind. I walk into Dutch's bedroom and it is dark. I ask him why? He might say, "Because I like a dark room," but I realize that he has simply learned to accept that it's going to be that way because he can't turn on the lamp anymore. So what can be done? We can design a lamp that lets him choose whether he wants it dark or not—a "sensor lamp" which turns on when its base is touched. Now he has control over his environment, at least in that one respect, and that means a lot to someone in his situation.

Once we become accustomed to viewing our environment in these terms, it is surprising how many small items follow the Darwinian pattern. I saw an advertisement for a set of handsome coffee mugs recently, and ordered them by mail. When they arrived, they were so heavy, and their handles designed in such a way, that I could barely manage them. *What if I were older, weaker, arthritic?* I wondered. *I would not have been able to use them at all.*

The solution to this problem is emphatically *not* to design two sets of products, one for the "young" and healthy and another for the *"old"* and faltering. That is both inefficient and subtly insulting to older consumers. Market research shows that older Americans do not like products or advertising campaigns which call attention to their infirmities or even to their differences from younger people.

The answer is to design products which are equally suitable for people of all ages and levels of strength and dexterity. This approach offers us a marvelous opportunity to design a better physical environment for all Americans. By designing with the needs of older consumers in mind, we will find that the inevitable result is better products for all of us.

If we replace our pots and pans with lighter-weight, easier-to-handle aluminum kitchenware, we do a service for grandparents, but we will also meet the needs of a child of ten who must carry a boiling pot of spaghetti. Or, conversely, if we design a knife and fork for the child who is learning to use his utensils, they can be used in a nursing home, where the older citizen who has been unable to feed himself because of arthritis can begin to regain confidence in this small way.

The use of "vertical shelving" (in which the tomato soup is shelved in a narrow strip, from bottom to top shelf, rather than in a longer horizontal row at a given height), helps not only the older shopper, but younger and shorter ones as well.

The point is that if a product or service works better for older people, it works better for everyone!

Corporate America, for the most part, has responded to the rising wave of older Americans with a big yawn. To date few companies have rushed to develop strategies for producing and marketing mainstream products for the older consumer with aggressive, meaningful compaigns.

Any big company should leap at an opportunity to cultivate a market share that makes 25 percent of all major appliance purchases, controls over 50 percent of all discretionary income, and 70 percent of whom own their own homes. That is exactly what the over-fifty population represents, and the companies which discover its potential will gain for themselves a loyal and lucrative group of customers.

I predict such major initiatives are just around the corner; and, once it begins, the trend will soon become a virtual stampede. In a few years, having product development and advertising campaigns aimed at older consumers will be obligatory for major corporations. It may be like having a Statue of Liberty commercial on television in 1985—everybody who is anybody must have one. That's how it will be with age-conscious marketing within a few years.

In all of this, there is a nice serendipity—an extra, incidental payoff—which is that we younger Americans will one day live in the world of older citizens which we now create. If we spend the effort to make this a better world for our parents and grandparents, one day, God willing, we will be on the receiving end of it.

In the long run, it's hard to improve on the simple application of the Golden Rule. Sooner or later, it all comes back.

# CHAPTER

## 21

I SOMETIMES CONDUCT WORKSHOP SESSIONS for young trainees who are preparing to become staff members in nursing homes. It is not unusual for these people to be nervous about how to treat elderly patients who will be in their charge.

"How should I act?" they ask me. "How should I talk?"

"How do you act with your friends?" I usually respond. "How do you talk to your friends?"

"Well, it's not the same!" they protest.

And I tell them it had better be the same, or very nearly so, or they may as well find another career. If they can't think of these older men and women as friends and peers, no amount of training will make the chemistry right between them.

As much as I enjoy working on better products and

services for the elderly, I realize that their most basic need is not for a more carefully designed environment as much as it is for a more sensitive and caring attitude from the general public.

Designers can do a much better job in creating suitable housing for the elderly, better individual units, more efficient apartments and townhouses, and certainly more aesthetically pleasing nursing homes and health-related facilities. But unless those places are staffed by individuals who see older citizens as persons of worth and value, life will continue to be a dreary prospect for many of them.

I receive mail from many people who hear of my work. One of the most touching letters I have ever read came from Yorkshire, England. It came from a nurse who works in a geriatric ward at Ashludie Hospital nearby. An *old* lady died in the ward, she explained, and another nurse going through her possessions found a poem she had written. The verses so impressed the staff that copies were duplicated and distributed to every nurse in the hospital. She enclosed a copy of the poem:

What do you see, nurses, what do you see?
Are you thinking when you are looking at me,
A crabby *old* woman, not very wise
Uncertain of habit, with faraway eyes.
Who dribbles her food and makes no reply,
When you say in a loud voice, "I do wish you'd
    try";
Who seems not to notice the things that you do,
And forever is losing a stocking or shoe.
Who uninteresting or not, lets you do as you will
With bathing and feeding the long day to fill.

Is that what you're thinking, is that what you
    see?
Then open your eyes, nurse, you're not looking at
    me.
I'll tell you who I am as I sit here so still,
As I rise at your bidding, as I eat at your will,

I'm a small child of ten with a father and mother,
Brothers and sisters who love one another.
A young girl of sixteen with wings on her feet,
Dreaming that soon now a lover she'll meet;
A bride soon at twenty, my heart gives a leap,
Remembering the vows I promised to keep.
At twenty-five now I have young of my own
Who need me to build a secure, happy home.
A woman of thirty my young now grow fast,
Bound to each other with ties that should last.
At forty my young sons have grown and are gone,
But my man's beside me to see I don't mourn.

At fifty once more babies play at my knee,
Again we know children, my loved one and me.
Dark days are upon me, my husband is dead.
I look at the future—I shudder with dread.
For my young are all rearing young of their own,
And I think of the years and the love that I've
    known.

I'm an *old* woman now, and nature is cruel;
'Tis her jest to make *old* people look like a fool.
The body it crumbles, grace and vigor depart,
There is now a stone where I once had a heart.
But inside this old carcass a young girl still
    dwells,
And now and again my battered heart swells.
I remember the joys, I remember the pain,
And I'm loving and living life over again.

I think of the years all too few, gone too fast;
And accept the stark fact that nothing can last.

So open your eyes, nurses—open and see,
Not a crabby *old* woman, LOOK CLOSER AT ME!

\* \* \* \*

I believe most of the elderly men and women we meet would say to us, in one way or another, "Open your eyes, and look closer at me!" Don't see the wrinkles, don't see the stereotypes; but take the time to look closely enough to see me for the person I am.

If I could wish for any particular result from my work, it would be that people of all ages would learn that we live in a community, a society; that we are not isolated; that we are all connected, the baby, the child, the teenager, the young adult, and the senior citizen—and we are responsible *to* one another and *for* one another.

People must hear that there is nothing to fear from each other. People must know they don't have to fear their own aging, or that of people they love. There is no reason to withdraw from each other, or to give up on oneself or on each other. There is no reason for the sixteen-year-old kid working at McDonald's to assume when older customers come to the counter that they will be deaf and difficult to deal with. There is no reason for that elderly couple to think that the kid behind the counter will be rude or abrasive or will not like them.

I had a marvelous, maybe even a unique opportunity. At an important passage in my own life, with the help of makeup and "antique" clothes, I was cata-pulted through the continuum we call the lifespan. And although I thought I was prepared for what I would see and feel, I was not. I don't think anyone could ever be.

What did I learn?

I learned to cherish every moment, savor every ex-perience, and grasp every opportunity.

I learned that the presence of God is equally as real, and equally as precious, at any age.

I learned that, after Him, people are the most impor-tant element in my life—that relationships are what matter most, and if they are right, we need not be overwhelmed by career and deadlines, pressures and fears, strange places and things.

And I was reminded of the ultimate importance of loving and caring and sharing.

It was a valuable lesson; a worthwhile journey.

# EPILOGUE

Much has changed in Pat Moore's life since that early morning in 1979 when she flagged a Manhattan cab to begin her journey to Columbus, Ohio, and into the world of aging Americans.

At that time she was already a highly respected industrial designer, and today that successful career continues. Her dream of owning and managing her own design firm has become a reality. In late 1981, she founded Moore and Associates, a thriving company specializing in age-related projects which capitalize on her expertise in gerontology.

Pat Moore seems always to have combined a pragmatic awareness of business realities with her softer, more sentimental side, and that fusion of heart and head is apparent in her leadership of Moore and Associates. Though the young company reflects her near-missionary zeal for the needs of older citizens, it also has managed to land solid contracts with some of the nation's biggest corporations, often in competition with firms which are larger and better established.

Her company has handled work for such giants as Johnson and Johnson; 3M; Kimberly-Clark; Merck, Sharp, and Dohme; Corning; and Bell Communications. As owner of her own business, Pat Moore's lifestyle has changed very little. She works long hours, travels extensively, answers her own phone, and generally maintains the same unpretentious style as when she was a junior designer at Loewy's ten years ago.

One thing which has changed, though, is the level of Pat Moore's public visibility. Her experiences in the character of an *old* woman have made her a symbol of the aging issue in this country and, along with it, something of a media star.

Since her work in character first came to public attention, interest in it has mushroomed. She has been invited to appear on such major national television programs as the "Today" show on NBC, "PM Magazine," ABC's "Nightline," and numerous others. Virtually every major newspaper in the country has interviewed her, including the New York *Times,* the Chicago *Tribune,* and the Seattle *Post.* She has been quoted in *Time* magazine, featured in *Reader's Digest, People,* and *Ladies Home Journal,* and sought for radio call-in shows by stations all over the dial. The rights to her story have been purchased for a made-for-TV movie.

In short, Pat Moore has become a full-blown media personality.

And how does she feel about all this attention? "I

don't really like it," she admits, wrinkling her nose. "It takes a lot of time, and it's very tiring. On the other hand, I am absolutely delighted to be able to talk about the issues of aging to such large audiences. I was caught offguard by the 'crusade' element, and I'm having to get comfortable with it. All I wanted to do was to be able to design concepts and products that fit the entire age range, not get up in front of large audiences and talk. But I'll have to admit, I like it when people come up to me after a presentation and tell me how I've opened their eyes or helped them . . . but . . ."

The ambivalence seems real. Pat Moore might well be happiest as an industrial designer, developing the ultimate packaging concept for a geriatric diet. But she is smart enough to know that her "cause" needs a media hero—or heroine—more than it needs another designer, and that she has become such a symbol, like it or not.

It would be difficult to imagine anyone more perfectly cast in the role of media spokesperson than Pat Moore. She is so attractive and youthful that she seems the physical antithesis of the population group whose interests she espouses. Her Bambi eyes and soft voice are disarming to the interviewer who expects a social-activist female more in the Bella Abzug mold; but when she begins to make her case, she is articulate and forceful, and it is obvious that she cares very deeply.

In her own style, despite her disclaimers, Pat Moore is very much the crusader. The Philadelphia *Inquirer* recently called her a "designer-as-spitfire."

Her bent toward social action is honestly come by—

it is something of a family trait, as she whimsically describes it. One of her earliest memories is of her father's private battle with a nationally known department store chain. It seems that he was dissatisfied with an auto battery which he bought from a local retail store, and even more dissatisfied with what he regarded as lack of proper response to his complaint. He called the family into the living room one night after dinner, made an angry speech about how the little man must not be abused by the giant corporation, and with great ceremony whipped out his charge card for that store and cut it in little pieces with a pair of scissors, while his wife and daughters tried to calm him down.

After that, Pat recalls, all members of the family were forbidden to shop at that store. It was a matter of principle. Mrs. Moore would occasionally sneak into the store to buy a favorite product or two, which she would carefully repackage in another bag before taking home. In the Moore household, causes were to be taken seriously!

The daughter learned her lesson well. Although she is not sounding a call for older Americans to chain themselves to the White House gates in protest of their treatment in this country, she does encourage them to be more vocal and energetic in pursuit of their rights. The problem, she says, is that the older generation has always placed such a premium on courtesy and mutual respect, that they are too trusting and not aggressive enough in situations in which someone clearly takes advantage of them or treats them with a lack of dignity.

Her message to older Americans who are reluctant

to protest shabby treatment: "You have to do it for yourself, and when you do it for yourself, you do it for everyone."

There is a certain irony in the fact that this symbol and standard-bearer for the rights of older citizens is a woman barely thirty-two years of age. It is an example of the very attitudes against which she speaks, that it takes a young woman to gain a media platform from which to address the needs of the elderly.

The popular attention which Pat has brought to the issues of agism has not prevented her from becoming a respected figure among gerontologists in professional and academic circles. To the contrary, serious researchers and scholars both honor and listen to her; she frequently is invited to address major national and regional conferences, and has spoken at the International Congress of Gerontology.

In her personal life, things have turned out equally well for Pat Moore. In June of 1985, she married her long-time friend and colleague, Daniel Formosa. The wedding took place at the main altar of Saint Patrick's Cathedral on Fifth Avenue, followed by a honeymoon trip down the River Nile in Egypt.

And what about the *Old* Pat Moore, the sweet *"old"* lady of eighty-five who lived, off and on, for three years on the streets and park benches of North America?

That version of Pat Moore is gone now. Her collection of gloves and jewelry fill a shoebox; her eyeglasses, lipstick, and hearing aid are tucked into a handbag; and her dresses and sweaters are folded and wrapped in a plastic bag. She has been reduced to a neat stack of clothing and boxes on the top shelf of a bedroom closet.

Toward the end of 1981, being in character became more and more painful for Pat, and the contacts she made were increasingly repetitive, yielding little new information. In April of 1982, she became the *old* woman for the last time. She took a stroll around the neighborhood, boarded a bus and went up to Bloomingdale's for a last visit there, walked down Fifty-ninth Street to Central Park for a final, familiar walk around the pond, and went home.

Does Pat Moore, the young one with the smooth skin and the pretty eyes, ever miss the *"old* lady"?

"Oh, I miss her," Pat answers without hesitation. "She was a good friend. We meant a great deal to each other, but for now we've said good-bye."

"It's not a sad parting, though," she adds with a mischievous smile, "I expect to see her again—in the mirror—in about fifty years!"